The
Retirement

The
Retirement Years

Ellen G. White

REVIEW AND HERALD® PUBLISHING ASSOCIATION
WASHINGTON, DC 20039-0555
HAGERSTOWN, MD 21740

Copyright © 1990 by
Ellen G. White Estate

PRINTED IN U.S.A.

95 94 93 92 91 90   10 9 8 7 6 5 4 3 2 1

R & H Cataloging Service

White, Ellen Gould (Harmon), 1827-1915.
   The retirement years.

   1. Retirement.   2. Elderly.   3. Old age.
I. Title.
                301.435

ISBN 0-8280-0584-2

THE RETIREMENT YEARS

A Compilation From the Writings of
Ellen G. White

Contents

THE HOW AND WHY
OF THIS BOOK

EVENTUALLY all of us reach the age when we must slow down a bit and turn over our work to younger hands and hearts. When that time comes, because of changing emotional, physical, and spiritual needs, some of us may need to secure help and counsel from experienced clergy, medical practitioners, and gerontologists. Fortunately, such help is abundant in the world today. Hundreds of helpful books, magazines, and lecture series are available for people fifty and above, and for retirement clubs now springing up around the world.

The presses of the Seventh-day Adventist Church have prepared several volumes aimed at senior readership, and all of them are good, but never before have the resources and help contained in the writings of Ellen G. White been brought together in a book aimed especially at the needs of senior citizens.

In the present volume Ellen White offers many inspired and inspiring answers to questions raised by golden-agers. These gems of thought have been gleaned from her letters, manuscripts, books, and periodical articles, many of which were written after she was 65—the 23 years from 1892-1915.

Ellen White lived life to the full until she was 87. At the age of 64, when most people are approaching retirement, she was serving in Australia as counselor and missionary, along with other stalwart pioneers of the church, to help gain a foothold for the Lord's work on that island continent.

In her newly built home on the campus of the School for Christian Workers (now Avondale College) she wrote her absorbing biography of Jesus' life on earth, *The Desire of Ages*. When she was not writing, she was preaching in the churches, meeting with conference committees, and offering counsel. When she urged, "Build a college after the Lord's pattern," Australasian Missionary College arose. Again, when she counseled, "Bring to birth a representative sanitarium in the suburbs of Sydney," a medical institution was built. In the creation of these institutions, church leaders revealed their faith in the inspired directions of the prophetic gift.

At the same time there poured forth from her facile pen a steady stream of inspirational articles and letters of counsel that found their way to church editors, leaders, and laymen, not only in Australia but in North America, Europe, and South America.

During the last fifteen years of her life (1900-1915) Mrs. White was back in the United States, living in her newly acquired "Elmshaven" home near St. Helena, California. While there she ardently hoped to enjoy a little of the ease and respite of retirement. But alas, the unique place that she occupied in the church as the Lord's special messenger made her the frequent and unrelenting object of demands from God's people for counsel and direction.

The servant of the Lord found it difficult to refuse these invitations, which included preaching appointments at camp meetings, conference sessions, and local churches. She journeyed eastward across the North American continent to speak at the 1909 General Conference session in Takoma Park when she was 82 years old.

And during the "Elmshaven" years nearly a dozen of her best books were published—*Education*; *The Ministry of Healing*; volumes 6, 7, 8, and 9 of the *Testimonies*; *The Acts of the Apostles*; *Counsels to Teachers, Parents, and Students*; *Gospel Workers*; *Life Sketches*; and finally (posthumously), *Prophets and Kings*.

Ellen White did not believe in "retirement by rust." To her, retirement was "by wear and tear." But she was not a hard taskmaster; rather, a mentor graced with an understanding heart and the merciful attitudes that she had gained by intimate acquaintance with a kind heavenly Father and His Son, Jesus Christ. For example, she counseled a workaholic preacher in his sunset years to be temperate in his labors, for he was killing himself by overwork. She encouraged him to grasp the thought that he had earned the privilege to relax, to ripen for heaven, and to enjoy some of the restful and peaceful moments of a happy retirement.

As Trustees it is our prayer that this collection of letters, articles, and messages from the pen of God's devoted servant will be a practical and cherished source of wisdom and guidance to people of retirement years, as well as to those of preretirement times who wish to grasp more fully the statement of Christ: "I am come that they might have life, and that they might have it more abundantly" (John 10:10).

Board of Trustees of the Ellen G. White Estate

ABBREVIATIONS OF SOURCES

AA	*The Acts of the Apostles*
AH	*The Adventist Home*
1BC	*The Seventh-day Adventist Bible Commentary,* vol. 1 (2BC, etc., for vols. 2-7)
DA	*The Desire of Ages*
Ed	*Education*
Ev	*Evangelism*
GCB	*General Conference Bulletin*
GW	*Gospel Workers*
LS	*Life Sketches*
Ms	Ellen G. White Manuscript
MH	*The Ministry of Healing*
PK	*Prophets and Kings*
PUR	*Pacific Union Recorder*
RH	*Review and Herald*
SD	*Sons and Daughters of God*
2SM	*Selected Messages,* book 2
ST	*Signs of the Times*
1T	*Testimonies for the Church,* vol. 1 (2T, etc., for vols. 2-9)
TM	*Testimonies to Ministers*
TSB	*Testimonies on Sexual Behavior, Adultery, and Divorce*
WM	*Welfare Ministry*

ADVENTIST PIONEERS

Respect the Aged Pioneers

TO the aged pioneer laborers who have been connected with the work of the third angel's message almost from its beginning, whose experiences in it date nearly from the passing of the time in 1844, the Lord says: "Your help is needed. Do not take upon yourselves loads that others who are younger can carry. It is your duty to be careful in your habits of life. You are to be wise in the use of your physical, mental, and spiritual strength. You who have passed through so many and such varied experiences are to do all that it is possible for you to do to preserve your powers, that you may labor for the Lord as long as He permits you to stand in your lot and place to help to advance His work.". . .

The cause needs the help of the old hands, the aged workers, who have had years of experience in the cause of God; who have watched the development and the progress of the message in its various lines; who have seen many go into fanaticism, cherishing the delusion of false theories, resisting all the efforts made to let the light of truth reveal the superstitions that were coming in to confuse minds and to make of none effect the message which in these last days must be given in its purity to God's remnant people.

Many of the tried servants of God have fallen asleep in Jesus. Let the help of those who are left alive to this day be appreciated. Let their testimony be valued. The good hand of the Lord has been with these faithful workers. He will uphold them by His strong arm, saying: "Lean on Me. I will be your strength and your exceeding great reward." Those who were in the message at its beginning, who fought bravely when the battle went hard, must not lose their hold now.

The most tender interest should be cherished toward those whose life interest is bound up with the work of God. Notwithstanding their many infirmities, these workers still possess talents that qualify them to stand in their lot and place. God desires them to occupy leading positions in His work. They have stood faithful amidst storm and trial, and are among our most valuable counselors. How thankful we should be that they can still use their gifts in the Lord's service!

Let not the fact be lost sight of that in the past these earnest wrestlers sacrificed everything to advance the work. The fact that they have grown old and gray in the service of God is no reason why they should cease to exert an influence superior to the influence of men who have far less knowledge of the work and far less experience in divine things. Though worn and unable to bear the heavier burdens that younger men can and should carry, their value as counselors is of the highest order. They have made mistakes, but they have learned wisdom from their failures; they have learned to avoid errors and dangers, and are they not then competent to give wise counsel? They have borne test and trial, and, though they have lost some of their vigor, they are not to be pushed aside by less-experienced workers, who know very little about the labor and self-sacrifice of these pioneers. The Lord does not thus lay them aside.

He gives them special grace and knowledge. . . .

As those who have spent their lives in the service of God draw near the close of their earthly history, they will be impressed by the Holy Spirit to recount the experiences they have had in connection with His work. The record of His wonderful dealings with His people, of His great goodness in delivering them from trial, should be repeated to those newly come to the faith. The trials also that have been brought on the servants of God by the apostasy of some once united with them in labor, and the working of the Holy Spirit to make of none effect the falsehoods told against those who were holding the beginning of their confidence firm unto the end, should be related.

The old standard-bearers who are still living should not be put in hard places. Those who served their Master when the work went hard, who endured poverty and remained faithful to the truth when our numbers were small, are ever to be honored and respected. I am instructed to say: Let every believer respect the aged pioneers who have borne trials and hardships and many privations. They are God's workmen and have acted a prominent part in the building up of His work.

The Lord desires the younger laborers to gain wisdom, strength, and maturity by association with the aged laborers who have been spared to the cause. Let the younger men realize that, in having such laborers among them, they are highly favored. Let them show great respect for the men of gray hairs, who have had long experience in the development of the work. Let them give them an honored place in their councils.

Old experiences should be told to others

God desires those who have come into the truth in later years to take heed to these words.

May the Lord bless and sustain our old and tried laborers. May He help them to be wise in regard to the preservation of their physical, mental, and spiritual powers. I have been instructed by the Lord to say to those who bore their testimony in the early days of the message: "God has endowed you with the power of reason, and He desires you to understand and obey the laws that have to do with the health of the being. Do not be imprudent. Do not overwork. Take time to rest. God desires you to stand in your lot and place, doing your part to save men and women from being swept downward by the mighty current of evil. He desires you to keep the armor on till He bids you lay it off. Not long hence you will receive your reward."—7T 286-289.

Vivid Memories of the Past

We arrived on the campground at Syracuse, New York, August 20. The next day, Thursday, we were glad to greet Elder U. Smith and wife. Here we met Elder Wheeler, with whom we became acquainted in New Hampshire thirty years ago. Here was Elder Cottrell, whom we have known for thirty years; Elder Taylor, for more than twenty-five years; Brother Robinson, for thirty-five years. My heart was touched as I looked upon these brethren who had long stood in defense of the faith.

More than a score of years have passed into eternity with their burden of record since these men became soldiers of the cross; but their experience in the early history of the cause of God has never grown dim. As their thoughts linger about the past, the fires of love and faith kindle anew in their hearts. They can say with John, "That which was from the beginning, which we have heard, which we have seen with our eyes, which we have looked upon, and our hands have handled, of the Word of life; . . . that which we have seen and heard declare we unto you, that ye also may have fellowship with us."

Others were present whom we highly esteem, tried friends of the cause, whom we have known many years. We saw their countenances light up with fresh assurance as they listened to the presentation of the truth which has kept their hearts warm all these years. These brethren and sisters have an accurate, personal knowledge of events that occurred a score or more years ago. Some of them have witnessed remarkable manifestations of the power of God in times of our greatest trial and need, when our numbers were few, when opposition was strong, and unreasonable objections had to be met. While things that occurred a week ago may be forgotten, these scenes of thrilling interest still live in the memory.

Whatever may be said of the later stages of their life-history, their earlier experience in this work has left traces which can never be erased. We cannot afford to let these aged sentinels drop out of sight. To many, by pen and voice, they have spoken precious words of truth; and they should still be encouraged to do all they can with their influence, their counsel, and their experience in the cause of God. More youthful workers are taking their place in active service, and this is right; but let these younger men keep a warm place in their hearts, and room in their councils, for those whose heads have grown gray in the service of Christ. We want to see these men keep on the armor, and press the battle to the gates. We want to see them share with younger soldiers the triumphs of the final victory. It will be joy indeed to see them, when the conflict is ended, crowned and honored among the victorious ones. —RH Oct. 28, 1884.

The Dead Still Speak

At half past two o'clock P.M. I spoke to a full house [at Adams Center, N.Y.]. . . . We were gratified to meet the aged servants of God on this occasion. We have been acquainted from the rise of the third angel's message with Elder [Frederick] Wheeler, who is now nearing eighty years. We have been acquainted with Elders [H. H.] Wilcox and [Chas. O.] Taylor for the last forty years. Age is telling on these old standard-bearers, as well as upon me. If we are faithful to the end the Lord will give us a crown of life that fadeth not away.

The aged standard-bearers are far from being useless and laid aside. They have a part to act in the work similar to that of John. They can say, [1 John 1:1-7 quoted].

This was the spirit and life of the message that John bore to all in his old age, when he was nearly one hundred years old. The standard-bearers are holding fast their banners. They are not loosening their hands on the banner of truth until they lay off the armor. One by one the old warriors' voices become silent. Their place is vacant. We see them no more, but they being dead yet speak, for their works do follow them. Let us treat very tenderly the few aged pilgrims remaining, esteeming them highly for their works' sake. As their powers are becoming worn and enfeebled, what they do say is of value. As precious testimony let their words be treasured. Let not the young men and the new workers discard or in any respect show indifference to the men of hoary hairs, but let them rise up and call them blessed. They should consider that they have themselves entered into these men's labors. We wish that there was much more of the love of Christ in the hearts of our believers for those who were first in the proclamation of the message. —2SM 223, 224.

Deep Appreciation for the First Burden-bearers

While you are anxious to do all that you possibly can, remember, Elder Haskell, that it is only by the great mercy and grace of God that you have been spared these many years to bear your testimony. Do not take upon yourself loads that others who are younger can carry. . . .

Many of the tried servants of God have fallen asleep in Jesus. We greatly appreciate the help of those who are left alive to this day. We value their testimony. Read the first chapter of First John, and then praise the Lord that notwithstanding your many infirmities you can still bear witness for Him. . . .

We can easily count the first burden-bearers now alive [1902]. Elder [Uriah] Smith was connected with us at the beginning of the publishing work. He labored in connection with my husband. We hope always to see his name in the *Review and Herald* at the head of the list of editors; for thus it should be. Those who began the work, who fought bravely when the battle went so hard, must not lose their hold now. They are to be honored by those who entered the work after the hardest privation had been borne.

I feel very tender toward Elder Smith. My life interest in the publishing work is bound up with his. He came to us as a young man, possessing talents that qualified him to stand in his lot and place as an editor. How I rejoice as I read his articles in the *Review*—so excellent, so full of spiritual truth. I thank God for them. I feel a strong sympathy for Elder Smith, and I believe that his name should always appear in the *Review* as the name of the leading editor. Thus God would have it. When, some years ago, his name was placed second, I felt hurt. When it was again placed first, I wept, and said, "Thank God." May it always be there, as God designs it shall be, while Elder Smith's right hand can hold a pen. And when the power of his hand fails, let his sons write at his dictation.

I am thankful that Elder [J. N.] Loughborough can still use his abilities and his gifts in God's work. He has stood faithful amid storm and trial. With Elder Smith, my husband, Brother Butler, who joined us at a later period, and yourself [S. N. Haskell], he can say, "That which was from the beginning, . . . that which we have seen and heard declare we unto you, that ye also may have fellowship with us: and truly our fellowship is with the Father, and with his Son Jesus Christ" (1 John 1:1-3). —2SM 224-226.

Reprint Articles of Pioneers

The messages that we have received from heaven are true and faithful. When one man strives to bring in new theories, which are not the truth, the ministers of God should bear clear warning against these theories, pointing out where, if received, they would lead the people of God. Those who have received the light of present truth should not be easily deceived, and readily led from the true path into strange paths. The watchmen are to be wide-awake to discern the outcome of all specious reasoning; for serious errors will be brought in to lead the people of God astray. . . .

When men come in who would move one pin or pillar from the foundation which God has established by His Holy Spirit, let the aged men who were pioneers in our work speak plainly, and let those who are dead speak also, by the reprinting of their articles in our periodicals. Gather up the rays of divine light that God has given as He has led His people on step by step in the way of truth. This truth will stand the test of time and trial. —Ms 62, 1905.

G. I. Butler a Most Valuable Laborer*

It is with feelings of satisfaction and of gratitude to God that we see Elder [G. I.] Butler again in active

---

* Elder Butler retired in 1888 and bought a farm in Florida, where he planted an orange grove. Because his wife became an invalid the next year, he stayed on in retirement 12 years longer. After her death in 1901 he was elected president of the Florida Conference. The next year, at the age of 68, he was elected president of the Southern Union Conference, an office he held for five years.

service. His gray hairs testify that he understands what trials are. We welcome him into our ranks once more, and regard him as one of our most valuable laborers.

May the Lord help the brethren who have borne their testimony in the early days of the message, to be wise in regard to the preservation of their physical, mental, and spiritual powers. I have been instructed by the Lord to say that He has endowed you with the power of reason, and He desires you to understand the laws that affect the health of the being, and to resolve to obey them. These laws are God's laws. He desires every pio-neer worker to stand in his lot and place, that he may do his part in saving the people from being swept downward to destruction by the mighty current of evil—of physical, mental, and spiritual declension. My brethren, He desires you to keep your armor on to the very close of the conflict. Do not be imprudent; do not overwork. Take periods of rest.

The church militant is not the church triumphant. The Lord desires His tried servants, as long as they live, to advocate temperance reform. Unfurl the temperance banner. Teach the people to practice strict temperance in all things, and to be champions in favor of obedience to physical laws. Stand firmly for God's truth. Exalt before the people the banner bearing the inscription, "Here is the patience of the saints: here are they that keep the commandments of God, and the faith of Jesus" (Rev. 14:12). . . .

A few of the old standard-bearers are still living. I am intensely desirous that our brethren and sisters shall respect and honor these pioneers. We present them before you as men who know what trials are. I am instructed to say, Let every believer respect the men who acted a prominent part during the early days of the message, and who have borne trials and hardships and many privations. These men have grown gray in service. Not long hence they will receive their reward. . . .

The Lord desires His servants who have grown gray in the advocacy of truth to stand faithful and true, bearing their testimony in favor of the law.

God's tried servants must not be put in hard places. Those who served their Master when the work went hard, those who endured poverty and remained faithful in the love of the truth when our numbers were small, are ever to be honored and respected. Let those who have come into the truth in later years take heed to these words. God desires all to heed this caution. — 2SM 226, 227 (Letter 47, 1902).

Grow Old Gracefully

Brother Butler, let us—you and Brother Haskell and I—grow old gracefully. He desires you to stand for Him as a light-bearer. Let us encourage one another. I am given messages to bear to the erring, but because of this, I do not lose my interest in the one reproved, but continue to encourage him.

"Love as brethren, be pitiful, be courteous." We need now, just now, the impartation of the Holy Spirit. The Lord Jesus has much to bear in dealing with us. He is hurt when we hurt one another. "Inasmuch as ye have done it unto one of the least of these my brethren," He says, "ye have done it unto Me." . . .

The aged ministers are to be carefully and tenderly treated. We cannot spare one of them. The Lord would have them help one another and rejoice in Him. These tried warriors are to strengthen the faith of the people of God by relating their experience in connection with the building up of His work. —Letter 111a, 1904.

Growing Older but Continuing to Testify

Dear Brother [G. I.] Butler:

. . . I greatly desire that the old soldiers, grown gray in the Master's service, shall continue to bear their testimony right to the point, that those younger in the faith may understand that the messages which the Lord gave us in the past are very important at this stage of the earth's history. Our past experience has not lost one jot of its force. I thank the Lord for every jot and tittle of the Sacred Word. I would not draw back from the hard parts of our experience.

You must not work beyond your strength. I suppose that in the future our experience will be varied; but I think that you and I, in growing old in the service of Christ, in doing His will, are obtaining an experience of the highest value and most intense interest.

The judgments of the Lord are in the land. We must work with wholehearted fidelity, putting the whole being into what we do to help others move forward and upward. Let us press the battle to the gates. Let us be ever ready to speak words of encouragement to the halting and the weary. We can walk safely only as we walk with Christ. Let nothing dampen your courage.

Help those with whom you come in contact to work with fidelity.

I hope that in the future I may meet you at some of our gatherings. You and I are among the oldest of those living who have long kept the faith. If we should not live to see our Lord's appearing, yet, having done our appointed work, we shall lay off our armor with sanctified dignity. Let us do our best, and let us do it in faith and hope. My heart is filled with gratitude to the Lord for sparing my life for so long. My right hand can still trace subjects of Bible truth without trembling. Tell all that Sister White's hand still traces words of instruction for the people. I am completing another book on Old Testament history [*Prophets and Kings*].

May the Lord bless you and keep you in hope and courage. — 2SM 229, 230 (Letter 130, 1910).

Guard Memory of Pioneers

As those who took up the work at the beginning of the message have advanced by self-denial and self-sacrifice, God has given them His blessing. They have had much to learn, they have made mistakes, they have needed continual guidance and counsel; but they have had reason for constant gratitude, because the work has gone forward in spite of poverty and a lack of facilities. They strained every nerve to make the work a success, to establish those buildings which were necessary for the proper development of the work; and under all circumstances the Lord guided them.

Those who enter the work later, to find things ready to their hand, should at least attempt to pay the debt they owe the Lord and the workers who went before them, by carrying the truth into new territories, until it has gone to every nation, kindred, tongue, and people. In every country men and women are to be raised up to carry forward the very work begun by those who have been laid away to rest. The memory of those pioneer workers is to be guarded, and from their treasure of experience the workers of today are to learn to pass from one line of advanced work to another, following the methods declared by the Holy Spirit to be in the order of God, asserting the principles enjoined in the Word, carrying the aggressive warfare into new fields. —GCB Third quarter, 1900, p. 164.

Avoid Criticism of the Pioneers

I saw that God is displeased with the disposition that some have to murmur against those who have fought the heaviest battles for them and who endured so much in the commencement of the message, when the work went hard.

The experienced laborers, those who toiled under the weight and the oppressive burdens when there were but few to help bear them, God regards; and He has a jealous care for those who have proved faithful. He is displeased with those who are ready to find fault with and reproach those servants of God who have grown gray in building up the cause of present truth. —3T 320, 321.

Let no one depreciate those who have been chosen of God, who fought manfully the battles of the Lord, who have woven heart and soul and life into the cause and work of God, who have died in faith, and who are partakers of the great salvation purchased for us through our precious sin-bearing, sin-pardoning Saviour. God has inspired no man to reproduce their mistakes, and to present their errors to a world that is lying in wickedness, and to a church composed of many who are weak in faith.

The Lord has not laid the burden upon men to revive the mistakes and errors of the living or the dead. He would have His laborers present the truth for this time. Speak not of the errors of your brethren who are living, and be silent as to the mistakes of the dead. Let their mistakes and errors remain where God has put them—cast into the depths of the sea. The less that is said by those who profess to believe present truth in regard to the past mistakes and errors of the servants of God, the better it will be for their own souls, and for the souls of those whom Christ has purchased with His own blood. —RH Nov. 30, 1897.

Let Us Encourage One Another*

I greatly desire that the old soldiers of the cross, those grown gray in the Master's service, shall continue to bear their testimony right to the point, in order that those younger in the faith may understand that the messages which the Lord gave us in the past are very important at this stage of the earth's history. Our past experience has not lost one jot of its force.

Let all be careful not to discourage the pioneers, or cause them to feel that there is little they can do. Their

---

* Drawn from Ellen White's second message to the General Conference session of 1913.

influence may still be mightily exerted in the work of the Lord. The testimony of the aged ministers will ever be a help and a blessing to the church. God will watch over His tried and faithful standard-bearers, night and day, until the time comes for them to lay off their armor. Let them be assured that they are under the protecting care of Him who never slumbers or sleeps; that they are watched over by unwearied sentinels. Knowing this, and realizing that they are abiding in Christ, they may rest trustfully in the providences of God.

I pray earnestly that the work we do at this time shall impress itself deeply on heart and mind and soul. Perplexities will increase; but let us, as believers in God, encourage one another. Let us not lower the standard, but keep it lifted high, looking to Him who is the Author and Finisher of our faith. When in the night season I am unable to sleep, I lift my heart in prayer to God, and He strengthens me and gives me the assurance that He is with His ministering servants in the home field and in distant lands. I am encouraged and blessed as I realize that the God of Israel is still guiding His people, and that He will continue to be with them, even to the end.

I am instructed to say to our ministering brethren, Let the messages that come from your lips be charged with the power of the Spirit of God. If ever there was a time when we needed the special guidance of the Holy Spirit, it is now. We need a thorough consecration. It is fully time that we gave to the world a demonstration of the power of God in our own lives and in our ministry.

The Lord desires to see the work of proclaiming the third angel's message carried forward with increasing efficiency. As He has worked in all ages to give victories to His people, so in this age He longs to carry to a triumphant fulfillment His purposes for His church. He bids His believing saints to advance unitedly, going from strength to greater strength, from faith to increased assurance and confidence in the truth and righteousness of His cause.

We are to stand firm as a rock to the principles of the Word of God, remembering that God is with us to give us strength to meet each new experience. Let us ever maintain in our lives the principles of righteousness, that we may go forward from strength to strength in the name of the Lord. We are to hold as very sacred the faith that has been substantiated by the instruction and approval of the Spirit of God from our earliest experience until the present time. We are to cherish as very precious the work that the Lord has been carrying forward through His commandment-keeping people, and which, through the power of His grace, will grow stronger and more efficient as time advances. The enemy is seeking to becloud the discernment of God's people, and to weaken their efficiency, but if they will labor as the Spirit of God shall direct, He will open doors of opportunity before them for the work of building up the old waste places. Their experience will be one of constant growth, until the Lord shall descend from heaven with power and great glory to set His seal of final triumph upon His faithful ones.

The work that lies before us is one that will put to

the stretch every power of the human being. It will call for the exercise of strong faith and constant vigilance. At times the difficulties that we shall meet will be most disheartening. The very greatness of the task will appall us. And yet, with God's help, His servants will finally triumph. "Wherefore," my brethren, "I desire that ye faint not" (Eph. 3:13) because of the trying experiences that are before you. Jesus will be with you; He will go before you by His Holy Spirit, preparing the way; and He will be your helper in every emergency. —2SM 406-408.

USEFULNESS OF OLDER WORKERS

Aged Workers Not Released From Service

I HOPE that none of those who have been long in the work will think that because they are growing old, they are incapacitated for service. I hope that they will stand up to bear their message as long as they have the evidence that the Lord is helping them. Edson [Ellen White's second son], encourage the men who have long borne burdens in our work. Even though in their old age their memory may fail somewhat, yet respect them, and the Lord will surely bless you. And let no aged worker, although he is old and gray, think that he is released from service. Let the work be carried on in simplicity. Surely we have the Lord on whom to depend. —Letter 102, 1910.

Older Workers Needed in Crises

God never leaves the world without men who can discern between good and evil, righteousness and unrighteousness. God has men whom He has appointed to stand in the forefront of the battle in times of emergency. In a crisis, He will raise up men as He did in ancient times. Young men will be bidden to link up with the aged standard-bearers, that they may be strengthened and taught by the experience of these faithful ones, who have passed through so many conflicts, and to whom, through the testimonies of His Spirit, God has so often spoken, pointing out the right way and condemning the wrong way. When perils arise, which try the faith of God's people, these pioneer workers are to recount the experiences of the past, when just such crises came, when the truth was questioned, when strange sentiments, proceeding not from God, were brought in.

The experience of those aged workers is needed now; for Satan is watching every opportunity to make of no account the old waymarks—the monuments that have been raised up along the way. We need the experience of the men who through evil report as well as through good report have been steadfast to the truth; men who have not built their house upon the sand, but upon the solid rock. —RH Nov. 19, 1903.

They Know How to Help Others

The aged standard-bearers in the cause of God are far from being useless. The men who have held the beginning of their confidence steadfast unto the end are not to be accounted second or third in the work of God. They are not to be cast aside as having outlived their usefulness. God has an important part for them to act in His work. By learning of Christ they have obtained a rich experience. When they have made false steps, they did not refuse to be corrected. When they wandered from the path that Christ trod, they allowed Him to lead them once more into it. Thus they have learned to help others. —MS 92, 1903.

Those who have grown old and gray in the service of God are not to be pushed aside by less experienced workers, who know very little about the labor and self-sacrifice of these pioneers. . . . Those who have such laborers among them are highly favored. Those who are commissioned by the Lord to do a large and important work, a work that will leave an impress for good or for ill on the world, according to the way in which it is done, need to seek counsel from those who have been instructed by the Lord. —MS 117a, 1901.

Aged Workers Give Wise Counsel

The most tender regard should be cherished for those whose life interest has been bound up with the work of God. These aged workers have stood faithful amid storm and trial. They may have infirmities, but they still possess talents that qualify them to stand in their place in God's cause. Though worn, and unable to bear the heavier burdens that younger men can and should carry, the counsel they can give is of the highest value.

They may have made mistakes, but from their failures they have learned to avoid errors and dangers, and are they not therefore competent to give wise counsel? They have borne test and trial, and though they have lost some of their vigor, the Lord does not lay them aside. He gives them special grace and wisdom.

Those who have served their Master when the work went hard, who endured poverty and remained faithful when there were few to stand for truth, are to be honored and respected. The Lord desires the younger laborers to gain wisdom, strength, and maturity by association with these faithful men. Let the younger men realize that in having such workers among them they are highly favored. Let them give them an honored place in their councils.

As those who have spent their lives in the service of Christ draw near to the close of their earthly ministry, they will be impressed by the Holy Spirit to recount the experiences they have had in connection with the work of God. The record of His wonderful dealings with His people, of His great goodness in delivering them from trial, should be repeated to those newly come to the faith. God desires the old and tried laborers to stand in their place, doing their part to save men and women from being swept downward by the mighty current of evil. He desires them to keep the armor on till He bids them lay it down. —AA 573, 574.

Special Grace and Knowledge

The Lord gives special grace and knowledge to the aged men who have had an experience in the work from its earliest history, and have watched it develop in its various lines of progress. Let these men be appreciated and respected. Let not the fact be lost sight of that in the past they have sacrificed everything to advance the work. Because they are growing old is no reason why they should cease to exert an influence superior to the influence of the men who have had far less study of the Word, far less experience in divine things, far less knowledge of the communications of Christ to His people.

I have been instructed that no indifference or disrespect is to be shown to these burden-bearing pioneers in the work. They are God's workmen, and have acted a prominent part in building up the work which today ought to bear the similitude of the pattern shown them in the mount. —MS 34, 1901.

Older Ministers to Speak at Camp Meetings

In 1890 I was given the following message to bear to our people:

"A mistake has been made in putting young men forward to speak at our camp meetings, before large congregations, when they had not the vital truths to present that were appropriate for the occasion. Precious time has been occupied by those who did not themselves know the true message for this time. Pioneers in the cause—men who had the bread of life to give to the people, men whose hearts and minds were filled with the vital truths needed by the hundreds and thousands of people assembled—have sat and listened to young preachers who could not do justice to the occasion. Not even half work was done in the presentation of the gospel message."

I am now called upon to present a similar message to our churches. Our aged ministering brethren are not to be over-taxed, but when they are at any of our churches, those in the church should remember that it is always courteous to ask them to speak. It is only showing these brethren the respect due them to say, "Brethren, you are older in the faith than we are. Have you not the word of the Lord for us at this time?"

The time of these workers is precious. They have words to speak that the people need. When they come among you, give them all the time that they can possibly fill. Make arrangements that will enable you to obtain all the help possible from them during their stay.

At our camp meetings, when large congregations assemble, the time given to public speaking should be occupied, as far as possible, by old, experienced workers, who have the word of the gospel to present. Do not place before the large congregation a young man who has not been proved. He may do his best, but his words will not have the weight of the words of men of gray hairs, who have been long in active service, and who, understanding the deep things of God, can present them with clearness and power.

It would be doing a young man a great wrong to place him before a large congregation before he had been proved. It would not leave the best impression on the minds of the hearers.

In our camp meetings call to the front men of long experience and of the very best talent—men who can impress hearts by bringing forth clearly the strong reasons of our faith; men who obey the words, "Stand therefore, having your loins girt about with truth, and having on the breastplate of righteousness; and your feet shod with the preparation of the gospel of peace; above all, taking the shield of faith, wherewith ye shall be able to quench all the fiery darts of the wicked. And take the helmet of salvation, and the sword of the Spirit, which is the word of God."

Our camp meetings are not held for the purpose of putting men on exhibition, of showing off their capabilities. The people come together to receive spiritual good. There are among them those who are thirsting for the water of life. Give them opportunity to drink until their thirst is quenched. Let them hear a message fraught with the love of God. Let them have opportunity of listening to men of ripe talent, men whom God has been educating and training. The minds of these men are filled with truth that the people need. Do not bring in men who have not been proved, while men sit by in silence who have the word of God burning in their souls, and who may never again have opportunity to bear the message given them. Give these tried warriors all the opportunities to speak that they can improve without overtaxing themselves; for they can present the truths that are the very pillars of our faith.

The younger ministers are not to think, because they are not called to speak to the large congregation, that there is nothing for them to do. There is work for all to do. Let them hold meetings in the smaller tents. Let the occupants of several tents meet in one tent for prayer and social meeting. In such meetings as these the younger ministers can do good service. Let them speak a few words right to the point, and then give those present an opportunity to speak. All our people should learn to bear witness for God in social meeting.

Let the younger ministers work for the children and youth, holding special meetings for them, and also putting forth personal efforts for them.

Let the old standard-bearers go from place to place, from meeting to meeting. Let our people have the benefit of their long experience. Let them speak the truth in all its force, but let them be sure that their feet are shod with the preparation of the gospel of peace. Let them present the truth, not in a way that will arouse the worst feelings of the human heart, but in love and tenderness and compassion. "If there be therefore any consolation in Christ, if any comfort of love, if any fellowship of the Spirit, . . . fulfil ye my joy, that ye be likeminded, having the same love, being of one accord, of one mind. Let nothing be done through strife or vainglory; but in lowliness of mind let each esteem other better than themselves."

To our people as a whole, and to our younger and less experienced workers, I am instructed to say, "Let it be plainly seen that you respect and honor our aged workers, the men of gray hairs, who have seen long and faithful service in the cause of God, and who are recognized and honored in the courts of heaven as laborers together with God. —Letter 152, 1903.

Experienced Workers Needed in the Home Field

Dear Brother and Sister Haskell:

. . . Today I had an interview with Elder Loughborough* in regard to his going to Australia. I told him that it appeared to me that we were sending too many from the home field. I told him that the churches needed the work that he could do. I advised him to delay his journey, and work for a while in the churches, encouraging and comforting them, and setting things in order. We see the need of the help of old, experienced laborers, who have been connected with the work almost from its beginning, whose experience

_____
* Elder J. N. Loughborough was 69 years old when this letter was written.

in it dates nearly from the passing of the time in 1844. We need the help of men who can testify as did John, "That which we have seen and heard declare we unto you."—Letter 195, 1901.

We cannot afford to deprive our home mission of the influence of middle-aged and aged ministers to send them into distant fields, to engage in a work for which they are not qualified, and to which no amount of training will enable them to adapt themselves. The men thus sent out leave vacancies which inexperienced laborers cannot supply.—RH July 17, 1883.

Old Age More Productive Than Youth

The true minister of Christ should make continual improvement. The afternoon sun of his life may be more mellow and productive of fruit than the morning sun. It may continue to increase in size and brightness until it drops behind the western hills. My brethren in the ministry, it is better, far better, to die of hard work in some home or foreign mission field, than to rust out with inaction. Be not dismayed at difficulties; be not content to settle down without studying and without making improvement. Search the Word of God diligently for subjects that will instruct the ignorant and feed the flock of God. Become so full of the matter that you will be able to bring forth from the treasure house of His Word things new and old.

Your experience should not be ten, twenty, or thirty years old, but you should have a daily, living experience, that you may be able to give to each his portion of meat in due season. Look forward, not backward. Never be obliged to tug at your memory in order to relate some past experience. What does that amount to today to you or to others? While you treasure all that is good in your past experience, you want a brighter, fresher experience as you pass along. Do not boast of what you have done in the past, but show what you can do now. Let your works and not your words praise you. Prove the promise of God that "those that be planted in the house of the Lord shall flourish in the courts of our God. They shall still bring forth fruit in old age; they shall be fat and flourishing; to shew that the Lord is upright: he is my rock, and there is no unrighteousness in him" (Ps. 92:13-15). Keep your heart and mind young by continuous exercise. — 2SM 221, 222.

Efficiency May Constantly Increase

Our ministers who have reached the age of forty or fifty years should not feel that their labor is less efficient than formerly. Men of years and experience are just the ones to put forth strong and well-directed efforts. They are specially needed at this time; the churches cannot afford to part with them. Such ones should not talk of physical and mental feebleness nor feel that their day of usefulness is over.

Many of them have suffered from severe mental taxation, unrelieved by physical exercise. The result is a deterioration of their powers and a tendency to shirk responsibilities. What they need is more active labor.

This is not alone confined to those whose heads are white with the frost of time, but men young in years have fallen into the same state and have become mentally feeble. They have a list of set discourses, but if they get beyond the boundaries of these they lose their soundings.

The old-fashioned pastor, who traveled on horseback and spent much time in visiting his flock, enjoyed much better health, notwithstanding his hardships and exposures, than our ministers of today, who avoid all physical exertion as far as possible and confine themselves to their books.

Ministers of age and experience should feel it their duty, as God's hired servants, to go forward, progressing every day, continually becoming more efficient in their work, and constantly gathering fresh matter to set before the people. Each effort to expound the gospel should be an improvement upon that which preceded it. Each year they should develop a deeper piety, a tenderer spirit, a greater spirituality, and a more thorough knowledge of Bible truth. The greater their age and experience, the nearer should they be able to approach the hearts of the people, having a more perfect knowledge of them.

Men are needed for this time who are not afraid to lift their voices for the right, whoever may oppose them. They should be of strong integrity and tried courage. The church calls for them, and God will work with their efforts to uphold all branches of the gospel ministry. —4T 269, 270.

Last Days May Be the Best*

Do not speak words that will irritate or offend. The Lord desires you to guard every point in your character. You can be a blessing in communicating to others your knowledge of the truth and of health reform. . . .

The Lord loves you, and He desires you to do with power the work given you. When speaking to the people, do not seek to present something original and new. Give short talks, right to the point, on practical subjects. Thus you can feed starving souls.

I feel anxious that in our old age we who have known the truth for so long shall become mellow in spirit and in our methods of labor; that we shall understand the simple, yet important and comprehensive truths of the third angel's message; and that we shall receive these truths in the love of God, and impart them to others.

My brother, you need not feel that you are too old to train your voice. You talk in too low a tone. Open your mouth and use your abdominal muscles in sending forth the sound. Just now you are excellently situated for learning to talk clearly and distinctly. When talking to the workmen, take in deep inspirations, and let your tones be full and round. Thus you will gain in health. Your delivery will improve, and your efforts to help the people will be crowned with success. . . .

---

* Written to a 68-year-old physician who was leading out in the establishment of a medical institution in Australia.

The Lord has not forsaken you. He desires you to grow in grace, to increase in ability to help the people. But if you interest them, you must speak right to the point, and you must stop before you think you are half through.

I cannot endure the thought of any of our aged believers decreasing in influence and efficiency. The Lord wants you to cooperate with Him in making all you can of yourself. If you will unite willingly with Him in this work, your last days will be your brightest and best. Heed the cautions that I have given you. Keep close to the clear lines of truth, and do not let your voice sink so low that the hearers can scarcely catch the sound. You will be much benefited healthwise if you will put forth determined effort to make your voice heard. It is a God-given duty to improve in speech, and this you can do if you will try with determination. —Letter 11, 1901.

ASSOCIATION
OF YOUNG WITH OLD

Laborers Together With God

CHILDREN should be so educated that they will sympathize with the aged and afflicted and will seek to alleviate the sufferings of the poor and distressed. They should be taught to be diligent in missionary work; and from their earliest years self-denial and sacrifice for the good of others and the advancement of Christ's cause should be inculcated, that they may be laborers together with God. —6T 429.

Many youth who have but little experience push themselves forward, manifest no reverence for age or office, and take offense if counseled or reproved. We have already more of these self-important ones than we want. God calls for modest, quiet, sober-minded youth, and men of mature age, who are well-balanced with principle, who can pray as well as talk, who will rise up before the aged, and treat gray hairs with respect. —RH Nov. 13, 1883.

God has especially enjoined tender respect toward the aged. He says, "The hoary head is a crown of glory, if it be found in the way of righteousness (Prov. 16:31). It tells of battles fought, and victories gained; of burdens borne, and temptations resisted. It tells of weary feet nearing their rest, of places soon to be vacant. Help the children to think of this, and they will smooth the path of the aged by their courtesy and respect, and will bring grace and beauty into their young lives as they heed the command to "rise up before the hoary head, and honor the face of the old man" (Lev. 19:32). — Ed 244.

Older Ministers Should Educate Younger Workers

God calls upon His aged servants to act as counselors, to teach the young men what to do in cases of emergency. Aged workers are to bear, as did John, a living testimony of real experience. And when these faithful workers are laid away to rest, with the words, "Blessed are the dead which die in the Lord" (Rev. 14:13), there should be found in our schools men and women who can take the standard and raise it in new places.

While the aged standard-bearers are in the field, let those who have been benefited by their labors care for and respect them. Do not load them down with burdens. Appreciate their advice, their words of counsel. Treat them as fathers and mothers who have borne the burden of the work. The workers who have in the past anticipated the needs of the cause do a noble work when, in the place of carrying all the burdens themselves, they lay them upon the shoulders of younger men and women, and educate them as Elijah educated Elisha.

David offered to God a tribute of gratitude for the divine teaching and guidance he had received. "O God, Thou hast taught me from my youth" (Ps. 71:17), he declared. Those who in the history of the message have borne the burden and heat of the day, are to remember that the same Lord who taught them from their youth, inviting them, "Take My yoke upon you, and learn of Me" (Matt. 11:29), and giving them the light of truth, is just as willing to teach young men and women today as He was to teach them.

It is wisdom for those who have borne heavy loads to come apart and rest awhile. These faithful workers should be relieved of every taxing burden. The work they can do as educators should be appreciated. The Lord Himself will cooperate with them in their efforts to teach others. They should leave the wrestling to those who are younger; the future work must be done by strong young men. The work is under the control of the Author and Finisher of our faith. He can and will give fitness to men of opportunity. He will raise up those who can fight His battles. He never leaves His work to chance. This work is a great and solemn one, and it is to go forward.

It is not God's will that the fathers in His cause should use up their remaining vitality in bearing heavy loads. Let the young men shoulder every responsibility they can, and fight manfully the good fight of faith. The Lord knows better whom to select to do His work than do the wisest men, however interested they may be. It is God who implants His Spirit in the hearts of young men, leading them to fight for Him against great odds. Thus He inspired Paul of Tarsus, who fought with all his entrusted capabilities for Heaven's revealed truth, against apostates who ought to have upheld him. God's servants will have today to meet the same difficulties that Paul met. This experience some have had who are now raising the banner of truth. It is such men who can stand in defense of the truth. If they continue to be learners, God can use them to vindicate His law.

Let not the aged workers think that they must carry all the responsibilities, all the loads. New fields of labor are constantly opening before us. Let the young men unite with experienced laborers who understand the Scriptures, who have long been doers of the Word, who have brought the truth into the practical life, relying upon Christ day by day, who seek the Lord as Daniel did. Three times a day Daniel offered his petitions to God. He knew that One mighty in counsel was the source of wisdom and power. The truth as it is in Jesus —the sword of the Spirit, which cuts both ways—was his weapon of warfare.

In word, in spirit, in principle, the men who have made God their trust are an example to the youth connected with them. These faithful servants of God are to link up with young men, drawing them with the cords of love because they are themselves drawn to them by the cords of Christ's love. —2SM 227-229.

Older Workers Encourage the Younger Ones

The Lord desires His people to make constant advancement. He rejoices when young men become imbued with His spirit, and gird on the armor, to engage in aggressive warfare. Let us always encourage young men and young women to make the most of their capabilities, to improve their talents to the utmost, remembering the words, "Let no man despise thy youth." We do not expect that they will never err in word or action, but if they will heed the reproofs of the Lord, and correct every mistake, they will make advancement.

As we see God raising up young men for His work, we rejoice to see them increasing in the fear of the Lord in proportion as they increase in the knowledge of the truth. Such ones will cultivate a reverence for God and for His sacred service.

Let the older workers encourage the younger ones, never speaking lightly or disparagingly of them.

Day by day the young student teacher is storing away a fresh supply of knowledge. His understanding is enlightened. He can say, "God has opened my eyes to behold wondrous things out of His Word." A sense of God's mercy and greatness makes him childlike in his submissiveness and his willingness to serve.

These teachers do not feel the repression they would feel in the presence of older teachers. Their hearts glow with the love of God. The students catch the spirit, the windows of the heart are opened heavenward, and songs of gratitude ascend from hearts that burn with the love of God. As the teachers and students seek to learn their duty, with an unfeigned desire to be conformed to the image of God, they gain power to conquer the stubbornness of a selfish will.

Oh, I can see wisdom in thoroughly converted young men and young women engaging in the work of teaching. As they give themselves fully to God, they will learn more and more of Him. . . .

We do not in any way underrate the older teachers. No; we would encourage older and younger teachers to labor for God. But I am seeking to show you that schools may be managed, and managed successfully, by men who are not the most advanced in years and experience.

God can work through young, humble men. Let none forbid them. Let the young, devoted followers of Christ say, "The love of Christ constraineth me." Moving upon minds with the force of the grace of Christ, this love casts aside all hindrances and barriers, exerting upon souls a compelling influence that leads them to give themselves to God in unreserved consecration.

My brother, let nothing you do or say weaken the hands of men who are doing their best, and who have succeeded in gaining success. —Letter 102, 1902.

Warm Friendship Between Eli and Samuel

The life of Samuel from early childhood had been a life of piety and devotion. He had been placed under the care of Eli in his youth, and the loveliness of his character drew forth the warm affection of the aged priest. He was kind, generous, diligent, obedient, and respectful. The contrast between the course of the youth Samuel and that of the priest's own sons was very marked, and Eli found rest and comfort and blessing in the presence of his charge. It was a singular thing that between Eli, the chief magistrate of the nation, and the simple child so warm a friendship should exist. Samuel was helpful and affectionate, and no father ever loved his child more tenderly than did Eli this youth. As the infirmities of age came upon Eli, he felt more keenly the disheartening, reckless, profligate course of his own sons, and he turned to Samuel for comfort and support.

How touching to see youth and old age relying one

upon the other, the youth looking up to the aged for counsel and wisdom, the aged looking to the youth for help and sympathy. This is as it should be. God would have the young possess such qualifications of character that they shall find delight in the friendship of the old, that they may be united in the endearing bonds of affection to those who are approaching the borders of the grave. —ST Oct. 19, 1888.

Paul Trained Timothy and Titus

Paul made it a part of his work to educate young men for the gospel ministry. He took them with him on his missionary journeys, and thus they gained an experience that later enabled them to fill positions of responsibility. When separated from them, he still kept in touch with their work, and his letters to Timothy and Titus are an evidence of how deep was his desire for their success. "The things that thou hast heard," he wrote, "commit thou to faithful men, who shall be able to teach others also."

This feature of Paul's work teaches an important lesson to ministers today. Experienced laborers do a noble work when, instead of trying to carry all the burdens themselves, they train younger men, and place burdens on their shoulders. It is God's desire that those who have gained an experience in His cause, shall train young men for His service.

The younger worker must not become so wrapped up in the ideas and opinions of the one in whose charge he is placed, that he will forfeit his individuality. He must not lose his identity in the one who is instructing him, so that he dare not exercise his own judgment, but does what he is told, irrespective of his own understanding of what is right and wrong. It is his privilege to learn for himself of the great Teacher. If the one with whom he is working pursues a course which is not in harmony with a "Thus saith the Lord," let him not go to some outside party, but let him go to his superior in office, and lay the matter before him, freely expressing his mind. Thus the learner may be a blessing to the teacher. —GW 102, 103.

OBLIGATION OF CHILDREN TO AGED PARENTS

Obligation Never Ceases

THE obligation resting upon children to honor their parents is of lifelong duration. If the parents are feeble and old, the affection and attention of the children should be bestowed in proportion to the need of father and mother. Nobly, decidedly, the children should shape their course of action even if it requires self-denial, so that every thought of anxiety and perplexity may be removed from the minds of the parents. . . .

Children should be educated to love and care tenderly for father and mother. Care for them, children, yourselves; for no other hand can do the little acts of kindness with the acceptance that you can do them. Improve your precious opportunity to scatter seeds of kindness. — AH 360.

Show Kindness Even to Unjust Parents

If children think that they were treated with severity in their childhood, will it help them to grow in grace and in the knowledge of Christ, will it make them reflect His image, to cherish a spirit of retaliation and revenge against their parents, especially when they are old and feeble? Will not the very helplessness of the parents plead for the children's love? Will not the necessities of the aged father and mother call forth the noble feelings of the heart, and through the grace of

Christ, shall not the parents be treated with kind attention and respect by their offspring? Oh, let not the heart be made as adamant as steel against father and mother! How can a daughter professing the name of Christ cherish hatred against her mother, especially if that mother is sick and old? Let kindness and love, the sweetest fruits of Christian life, find a place in the heart of children toward their parents. . . .

Especially dreadful is the thought of a child turning in hatred upon a mother who has become old and feeble, upon whom has come those infirmities of disposition attendant upon second childhood. How patiently, how tenderly, should children bear with such a mother! Tender words which will not irritate the spirit should be spoken. A true Christian will never be unkind, never under any circumstances be neglectful of his father or mother, but will heed the command, "Honor thy father and thy mother." God has said, "Thou shalt rise up before the hoary head, and honor the face of the old man." . . .

Children, let your parents, infirm and unable to care for themselves, find their last days filled with contentment, peace, and love. For Christ's sake let them go down to the grave receiving from you only words of kindness, love, mercy, and forgiveness. —AH 362, 363.

Caring for Aged Parents Is a Privilege

The best way to educate children to respect their father and mother is to give them the opportunity of seeing the father offering kindly attentions to the mother, and the mother rendering respect and reverence to the father. It is by beholding love in their parents, that children are led to obey the fifth commandment.

After children grow to years of maturity, some of them think their duty is done in providing an abode for their parents. While giving them food and shelter, they give them no love or sympathy. In their parents' old age, when they long for expression of affection and sympathy, children heartlessly deprive them of their attention. There is no time when children should withhold respect and love from their father and mother. While the parents live, it should be the children's joy to honor and respect them. They should bring all the cheerfulness and sunshine into the life of the aged parents that they possibly can. They should smooth their pathway to the grave. There is no better recommendation in this world than that a child has honored his parents, no better record in the books of heaven than that he has loved and honored father and mother.

Let children carefully remember that at the best the aged parents have but little joy and comfort. What can bring greater sorrow to their hearts than manifest neglect on the part of their children? What sin can be worse in children than to bring grief to an aged, helpless father or mother? Those who grieve their aged parents are written in the books of heaven as commandment breakers, as those who do not reverence the God of heaven, and unless they repent and forsake their evil ways, they will not be found worthy of a place in the saints' inheritance. . . .

The thought that children have ministered to the comfort of their parents is a thought of satisfaction all through the life, and will especially bring them joy when they themselves are in need of sympathy and love. Those whose hearts are filled with love will regard the privilege of smoothing the passage to the grave for their parents an inestimable privilege. They will rejoice that they had a part in bringing comfort and peace to the last days of their loved parents. To do otherwise than this, to deny to the helpless aged ones the kindly ministrations of sons and daughters, would fill the soul with remorse, the days with regret, if our hearts were not hardened and cold as a stone.

Our obligation to our parents never ceases. Our love for them, and theirs for us, is not measured by years or distance, and our responsibility can never be set aside. —RH Nov. 15, 1892.

A Matter of Vital Importance

I was shown that you do not possess that filial love which you should. The evil in your nature is exercised in a most unnatural way. You are not tender and respectful to your parents. Whatever may be their faults, you have no excuse for the course you have pursued toward them. It has been most unfeeling and disrespectful. Angels turned from you in sadness, repeating these words: "That which ye sow ye shall also reap." Should time continue, you would receive from your children the same treatment which your parents have received from you. You have not studied how you could best make your parents happy, and then sacrificed your wishes and your pleasure to this end. Their days upon earth are few at most, and will be full of care and trouble even if you do all you can to smooth their passage to the grave.

"Honor thy father and thy mother: that thy days may be long upon the land which the Lord thy God giveth thee." This is the first commandment with promise. It is binding upon childhood and youth, upon the middle-aged and the aged. There is no period in life when children are excused from honoring their parents. This solemn obligation is binding upon every son and daughter, and is one of the conditions to their prolonging their lives upon the land which the Lord will give the faithful. This is not a subject unworthy of notice, but a matter of vital importance. The promise is upon condition of obedience. If you obey, you shall live long in the land which the Lord your God gives you. If you disobey, you shall not prolong your life in that land. —2T 80, 81.

CARE OF THE AGED

Institutions Not the Best Plan

MEN should not be employed to give their time and talents to the work of bringing the aged or the orphans together into a company to be fed and clothed. This is not the best way to manage these cases. . . .

Nor is it best to erect buildings for old men and old women, that they may be in a company together. Let them be helped in the very places where they can be helped. Let relations take care of their own poor relations, and let the church take care of its own needy members. This is the very work God would have the church do, and they will obtain a blessing in doing it. —WM 238.

The matter of caring for our aged brethren and sisters who have no homes is constantly being urged. What can be done for them? The light which the Lord has given me has been repeated: It is not best to establish institutions for the care of the aged, that they may be in a company together. Nor should they be sent away from home to receive care. Let the members of every family minister to their own relatives. When this is not possible the work belongs to the church, and it should be accepted both as a duty and as a privilege. —6T 272.

At nine o'clock we meet in the large tent with a few of the brethren to talk over the matter which is constantly urged upon us—that of the aged people who have no homes. What will be done with them?

The light that the Lord has given me was repeated:

Let every family take care of its own relatives, making suitable provision for them. If this is not possible, then the church should bear the burden. The Lord will bless His church in exercising benevolence. They are God's poor, and are not to be left unhappy and destitute.

If the church cannot do this, then the conference must take it up and make provision for the Lord's needy ones. —2SM 331.

Should Remain Among Friends

The aged also need the helpful influences of the family. In the home of brethren and sisters in Christ can most nearly be made up to them the loss of their own home. If encouraged to share in the interests and occupations of the household, it will help them to feel that their usefulness is not at an end. Make them feel that their help is valued, that there is something yet for them to do in ministering to others, and it will cheer their hearts and give interest to their lives.

So far as possible let those whose whitening heads and failing steps show that they are drawing near to the grave remain among friends and familiar associations. Let them worship among those whom they have known and loved. Let them be cared for by loving and tender hands.

Whenever they are able to do so, it should be the privilege of the members of every family to minister to their own kindred. When this cannot be, the work belongs to the church, and it should be accepted both as a privilege and as a duty. All who possess Christ's spirit will have a tender regard for the feeble and the aged.

The presence in our homes of one of these helpless ones is a precious opportunity to cooperate with Christ in His ministry of mercy and to develop traits of character like His. There is a blessing in the association of the old and the young. The young may bring sunshine into the hearts and lives of the aged. Those whose hold on life is weakening need the benefit of contact with the hopefulness and buoyancy of youth. And the young may be helped by the wisdom and experience of the old. Above all, they need to learn the lesson of unselfish ministry. The presence of one in need of sympathy and forbearance and self-sacrificing love would be to many a household a priceless blessing. It would sweeten and refine the home life, and call forth in old and young those Christlike graces that would make them beautiful with a divine beauty and rich in heaven's imperishable treasure. —MH 204, 205.

Ellen White's Care for Her Parents*

My children are as well as usual. Father and Mother are living with us, and they seem so contented and happy. They take care of their room, but eat with us. You don't know what a weight of care is removed from me, since I can watch over these two aged children. Mother does just as I wish her to, follows every suggestion I make. I dress her up neat as wax, comb her hair, and she looks like a nice, venerable old lady. Father also

---

* Robert and Eunice Harmon, Ellen White's parents, lived for a time with James and Ellen White in their home on Wood Street in Battle Creek, Michigan. Later, they occupied the house next door. Across the street was the home of James White's parents, Deacon John White and his wife. James and Ellen were most attentive to the needs of these godly people, all four of whom accepted the Adventist faith.

tries to please us in every way. We fix him up and he looks real nice.

I would give my love to all your family, especially your parents. Let us hear from you often. Don't sink down in despondency and doubt. Look up, be of good cheer, and God will lead us on to victory. —Letter 27, 1861 (To Lucinda Hall).

Help for a Former Brother-in-law

Dear Brother and Sister [Stephen] Belden:*
    Be assured that I do not forget you. I pray for you, that the Lord will open up ways whereby you will be enabled to do good on Norfolk Island. I shall try to send you some money now and then. All that I have sent you since coming to this country has been hired on interest, but while I live, I will care for you. May the Lord give you peace and comfort. He is our only Hope and our only Helper. I shall be glad to hear from you as often as you can write, and I will write to you as often as I can. When it is not possible for me to write I will communicate to you through others. In this mail I will send you copies of letters I have written to the brethren in Australia. —Letter 146, 1902.

    I gave Stephen Belden several hundred dollars. I could not let him and his wife suffer for food and clothing. I paid their expenses to and from Norfolk Island. —Letter 258, 1903 (To Lucinda Hall).

    I am sending you with this copies of letters in which

---

* Stephen Belden married Sarah Harmon, Ellen White's sister. Frank E. Belden, the well-known hymn writer, was their son. Sarah died in 1868. Stephen was living with his third wife on Norfolk Island, northeast of Australia, when these letters were written.

you may be interested. I wish I could talk with you both. I wish to ask you, Do you receive the two dollars a week that I arranged to have sent you by the Australian Union Conference? Please tell me in regard to this. Brother Hindson says that generally the money has been placed to your credit on the Office books, and that you have sent to the Office orders for goods, which have been filled. Would you prefer to have the money sent you? If so, please let this be known, and it will be done.

I made the arrangement before leaving Australia that you were to receive a certain sum each week. The brethren gave me their word that they would do as I had requested. Please let me know your circumstances, and if the arrangement that I made has not been carried out, I will write again about it. I do not want you to suffer for want of food and clothing.

It is not right that Frank does not write to you often. I am very sorry that he does not do this, and that he does not give you any financial help. Be assured that you shall not want while I live, if you will keep me acquainted with your circumstances. If your children neglect their duty, I will try to supply the lack, though I am paying interest on twenty thousand dollars.

Please write to me every mail. In the last mail I sent a response to your question regarding your coming to America. I dare not take the responsibility of deciding this matter. You can do as you think best, and as your friends shall decide. I dare not at my age take any more responsibility. I have very heavy burdens to bear in connection with the cause of God. Morning after morning I rise at one and two o'clock, to write out

important matters. —Letter 41, 1905 (To Brother and
Sister Stephen Belden).

In every mail that goes to Australia I send a letter to
Stephen Belden, with copies of letters that I have written to others. If I happen to miss a mail, he feels this
deeply. Just now I am sending him all that I can; for I
fear that each mail that goes will be the last in which I
can send him anything. Poor man, he is dying of cancer, and I am so far away that I cannot be near to help
him. But I can write to him, and I can pray for him.
—Letter 348, 1906.

Comfort for Stephen Belden's Widow

I know that poor Stephen must have suffered severely, but let us be thankful that the end came quietly.
Of him the words apply: "Here is the patience of the
saints: here are they that keep the commandments of
God, and the faith of Jesus. And I heard a voice from
heaven saying unto me, Write, Blessed are the dead
which die in the Lord from henceforth: Yea, saith the
Spirit, that they may rest from their labors: and their
works do follow them. And I looked, and behold a
white cloud, and upon the cloud one sat like unto the
Son of man, having on His head a golden crown, and in
His hand a sharp sickle. And another angel came out of
the temple, crying with a loud voice to Him that sat on
the cloud, Thrust in Thy sickle, and reap: for the time is
come for Thee to reap; for the harvest of the earth is
ripe" (Rev. 14:12-15).

These scenes will soon transpire, and then we shall

better understand the words, "Blessed are the dead which die in the Lord."

You may now rejoice in the thought that Stephen is free from all pain. There need be no more worry or anxiety on his account.

I am glad to know that our brethren in Australia do not forget you, that they have promised that you shall be cared for, whether you remain on the island, or whether you go to friends elsewhere. May the Lord bless and strengthen you and help you to recover from the long strain that has been upon you. Please continue to write to me by every mail that leaves Norfolk Island. —Letter 393, 1906 (To Mrs. Vina Belden, Dec. 16, 1906).

Fund for the Older Workers*

Some provision should be made for the care of ministers and others of God's faithful servants who through exposure or overwork in His cause have become ill and need rest and restoration, or who through age or loss of health are no longer able to bear the burden and heat of the day. Ministers are often appointed to a field of labor that they know will be detrimental to their health; but, unwilling to shun trying places, they venture, hoping to be a help and a blessing to the people. After a time they find their health failing. A change of climate and of work is tried, without bringing relief; and then what are they to do?

These faithful laborers, who for Christ's sake have

---

* In 1911, nine years after this counsel was published, a fund was created to care for the aged, sick, and infirm ministers. This pension program has expanded through the years to include financial assistance to a broad spectrum of retired church employees.

given up worldly prospects, choosing poverty rather than pleasure or riches; who, forgetful of self, have labored earnestly to win souls to Christ; who have given liberally to advance various enterprises in the cause of God, and have then sunk down in the battle, wearied and ill, and with no means of support, must not be left to struggle on in poverty and suffering, or to feel that they are paupers. When sickness or infirmity comes upon them, let not our workers be burdened with the anxious query: "What will become of my wife and little ones, now that I can no longer labor and supply their necessities?" It is but just that provision be made to meet the needs of these faithful laborers and the needs of those who are dependent on them.

Generous provision is made for veterans who have fought for their country. These men bear the scars and lifelong infirmities that tell of their perilous conflicts, their forced marches, their exposure to storms, their suffering in prison. All these evidences of their loyalty and self-sacrifice give them a just claim upon the nation they have helped to save—a claim that is recognized and honored. But what provision have Seventh-day Adventists made for the soldiers of Christ?

Our people have not felt as they should the necessity of this matter, and it has therefore been neglected. The churches have been thoughtless, and, though the light of the word of God has been shining upon their pathway, they have neglected this most sacred duty. The Lord is greatly displeased with this neglect of His faithful servants. Our people should be as willing to assist these persons when in adverse circumstances as they have been willing to accept their means and services when in health.

God has laid upon us the obligation of giving special attention to the poor among us. But these ministers and workers are not to be ranked with the poor. They have laid up for themselves a treasure in the heavens that faileth not. They have served the conference in its necessity, and now the conference is to serve them. When cases of this kind come before us, we are not to pass by on the other side. We are not to say, "Be ye warmed and filled" (James 2:16), and then take no active measures to supply their necessities. This has been done in the past, and thus in some cases Seventh-day Adventists have dishonored their profession of faith and have given the world opportunity to reproach the cause of God.

It is now the duty of God's people to roll back this reproach by providing these servants of God with comfortable homes, with a few acres of land on which they can raise their own produce and feel that they are not dependent on the charities of their brethren. With what pleasure and peace would these worn laborers look to a quiet little home where their just claims to its rest would be recognized!

The duty we owe to these persons has been referred to again and again, but no decided action has been taken in reference to it. As a people we should feel our responsibility in this matter. Every church member should feel an interest in all that concerns the human brotherhood and the brotherhood in Christ. We are members one of another; if one member suffers, all the members suffer with him. Something must be done, and the conference should have spiritual discernment, that they may understand the privileges and comforts that these worn-out workers need and deserve.— 7T 290-292.

CAUTIONS FOR AGING PERSONS

Age No Excuse for Relaxing Self-Discipline

I HAVE heard those who have been in the faith for years say that they used to be able to endure trial and difficulty, but since the infirmities of age began to press upon them, they had been greatly distressed when brought under discipline. What does this mean? Does it mean that Jesus has ceased to be your Saviour? Does it mean that when you are old and gray-headed, you are privileged to display unholy passion? Think of this. You should use your reasoning powers in this matter, as you do in temporal things. You should deny self, and make your service to God the first business of your life. You must not permit anything to disturb your peace. There is no need of it; there must be a constant growth, a constant progress in the divine life.

Christ is the ladder that Jacob saw, whose base rests upon the earth, and whose topmost round reaches into the highest heaven; and round after round, you must mount this ladder until you reach the everlasting kingdom. There is no excuse for becoming more like Satan, more like human nature. God has set before us the height of the Christian's privilege, and it is "to be strengthened with might by His Spirit in the inner man; that Christ may dwell in your hearts by faith; that ye, being rooted and grounded in love, may be able to comprehend with all saints what is the breadth, and length, and depth, and height; and to know the love of Christ, which passeth knowledge,

that ye might be filled with all the fulness of God"
(Eph. 3:16-19). —2SM 222, 223.

Be Content Where You Are

Dear Brother and Sister [Sawyer]:

In the night I seemed to be conversing with you,
and saying, The lesson you need to learn is to be restful
in the Lord. If you encourage a spirit of uneasiness and
discontent, you will mar your religious experience.

You are neither of you fitted to engage in missionary
work in some far-off field, for you have not the endur-
ance to overcome the difficulties you would meet in
such circumstances. If you cannot find missionary work
to do where you are, you will not be making the right
move to go to a place where you are not known in order
to do it. You will spend all the little money you have,
and then not be able to earn more.

I wish to say to you, Be content where you are. Gain
the mastery over your own minds. The uneasiness that
you allow yourselves to have disqualifies you to be a
blessing where you are. You have a home where you are;
enjoy your home, and thank the Lord that both your
lives are spared. Be thankful for the health you have.
North Carolina is not so good a place for you as California. You are engaging in missionary work by doing the
home work in a peaceable, contented spirit, in keeping
your clothing neat and presentable, and in cultivating
tidiness, holding yourself in readiness, when opportunity offers, to speak words of cheer to those who need
encouragement and help.

You will certainly be disappointed if you carry out

the plans you have in mind. You cherish the idea that you are not appreciated where you are. I ask you to put away this impression. Lay off this supposed responsibility to do missionary work in another field. You have reason to be thankful for the health and strength that is given you; but if you permit yourselves to be unhappy, you disqualify yourselves for the missionary work that you might do at home. You can be a blessing to each other and to those about you. Be cheerful and happy right where you are; cultivate the peace of God in your hearts. Do not be discouraged, but let your words be such as to inspire hope and good cheer, and your influence be of a character to uplift. May the Lord bless you and guide you, is my prayer.

Your age is sufficient reason why you should be contented where you are. Let the young men and women fill the hard places; it is your privilege to make your life as easy and comfortable as possible, while you prepare to move to a better country, even a heavenly. If the Lord sees that it is best that you work in the cause, He will open ways for you in California. Wait until the Lord makes your way clear. He would not have you left dependent on strangers in a far country. Be contented to sustain yourselves where you are, doing what you can for the cause of God. Help where you can with the word of your testimony, but do not feel that it is your duty to use up what little means you have in going to a new field.

I have written you my mind about this matter. I sincerely hope that you will be contented to stay where you are and enjoy your little home in peace and happiness. There is no reason why you should not enjoy the peace of Christ and His precious grace every day. I ask you not to place yourselves where your trials will be tenfold heavier than they now are. I have a special interest in your case, and pray that you will let the Lord mold and fashion you for the future, immortal life. — Letter 326, 1908.

Maintaining Personal Tidiness

Dear Brother Robert and Sister Hannah [Sawyer]:

I have received your letter, and will now reply. Lest I may have been misunderstood, I will say that I never intended that any counsel I have given you in the past should influence you against making any move that would be for your best interests. I have nothing to say to hinder your investing your means in any place where you could have better accommodations or advantages than you have where you now are.

But do not, I beg of you, move blindly. Do not place yourselves where you might be left destitute of means among strangers. For you to move to North Carolina I would consider ill-advised and inconsistent. I believe that no one who understands your circumstances would advise such a move. You need to act wisely and carefully. The Lord will not leave you, if you commit your case fully to Him.

I have words of counsel for Brother Robert. There is need of a reformation in your habits of dress and appearance. Untidiness in dress brings a reproach against the truth we profess to believe. You should consider that you are a representative of the Lord Jesus Christ. Let the whole life be in harmony with Bible truth. [Matt. 5:13-16, quoted.]

Neglect of your apparel has been a decidedly objectionable feature of your character. The impression you have made upon the minds both of believers and of unbelievers has not met the mind of the Spirit of God. Because of your slackness in this matter, our people have not felt free to advise you to take up work in selling literature, a work in which you might have accomplished much good. There is a useful work in which you might engage, visiting from house to house and speaking the right words, but your untidy influence works counter to the precious influence you might otherwise exert.

Remember that you can do an acceptable work for the Lord, but your personal appearance must be such as will recommend you as one who is letting his light shine for the Master. Will you not now take hold of this matter, and seek to effect a reformation in dress and appearance? If you should be entrusted with public work in our religious gatherings, with your lax ideas as to proper dress, you would not have the best influence over those whom you were trying to help.

This is not a matter of but little consequence, for it affects your influence over others for time and for eternity. You cannot expect the Lord to give you the fullest success in winning souls for Him unless your whole manner and appearance is of a nature that will win respect. The truth is magnified even by the impression of neatness in dress, and I know that you desire to use every jot of your influence on the side of the Master.

I have dwelt upon this matter because this is a decided defect in your character. The Lord has not been glorified by your laxness in dress. It may seem to be but a small matter, but it is against the honor and glory of God. Men and women who are rich in grace and the influence of holiness will be circumspect in every matter that helps to give them influence. Your present and future usefulness in the service of the Master depends in a measure upon how you relate yourself to this matter. We are nearing the close of time, and we must do all in our power to win souls for Christ's kingdom. —Letter 336, 1908.

Shun Overwork and Distrust of Brethren

Now, Brother Haskell, I suppose that you are in California and that you will find much work to do. I hope that health will be granted to you, but be careful not to overwork. You know that your head will not bear much perplexity, therefore shun this, and do not load down with responsibilities that others should carry. If your brethren seek to save you from overwork, do not mistrust their efforts. Do not think that it is because they have not confidence in you that they put some of the responsibilities upon others; for this will make you wretched. "Thinketh no evil," is one of the blessed attributes of Jesus Christ.

Your case has been laid open before me, and I know from what has been presented, that you spend many hours of grief and despondency because you think your brethren simply tolerate you but do not put confidence in you and trust you. It would not be right for them to act toward you as they have acted toward Elder Butler. Men have placed him where God should be placed, and by so doing have ruined their own religious experience and have also ruined Elder Butler, and the church was becoming strengthless, Christless because they glorified men when every jot of glory should be given to God. . . . Beware of Satan's devices. Nothing can weaken and unbalance the human mind like brooding over supposed wrongs, thinking that you are not appreciated. . . .

I greatly desire that you shall have a trustful mind, that you shall not depend upon your past confidence in God, but have a present, fresh faith, and maintain your confidence without wavering. Your soul must daily be warmed and invigorated by the truth of the gospel, and you refreshed by a daily living and new experience. I want you to have comfort and hope and joy in the Holy Ghost. Never, never feel the slightest disturbance because the Lord is raising up youth to lift and carry the heavier burdens and proclaim the message of truth. —Letter 14, 1891.

"Be Not Accusers of the Brethren"

I am bidden to say to my aged brethren, walk humbly with God. Be not accusers of the brethren. You are to do your appointed work under the direction of the God of Israel. The inclination to criticize is the greatest danger of many. The brethren whom you are tempted to criticize are called to bear responsibilities which you could not possibly carry; but you can be their helpers. You can do great service to the cause if you will, by presenting your experience in the past in connection with the labors of others. The Lord has not given to any of you the work of correcting and censuring your brethren. . . .

Follow on with your brethren to know the Lord. Sympathize with those who are bearing a heavy load, and encourage them wherever you can. Your voices are to be heard in unity, and not in dissension. — Ev 106, 107.

Aged Not to Labor in Cities

Feeble or aged men and women should not be sent to labor in unhealthful, crowded cities. Let them labor where their lives will not be needlessly sacrificed. Our brethren who bring the truth to the cities must not be obliged to imperil their health in the noise and bustle and confusion, if retired places can be secured. —Ev 71, 72.

Avoid "Shut-in Religion"

Dear afflicted brother:

We assure you that we sympathize with you in your affliction and in your sufferings. . . .

The old soldier on the field of battle frequently in his zeal exposes himself to danger and to death. He cannot do otherwise and have the assurance that he is doing his whole duty. This is found to be applicable in the service of the heavenly King. Wounds and bruises are received because Christ's soldiers, not willing to be in seclusion and inactivity, will not forsake their post of duty and be satisfied with a shut-in religion, [saying], "I am saved," and leave the world, and sinners in the world, to perish. . . .

My brother, I do not feel to give you one word of censure, saying you were independent, overzealous. I would have done just as you did. Had you foreseen all, you might have saved yourself much suffering; but you did not see, and you acted out your zeal and devotion to the cause of truth, and some others may be responsible for not doing their duty. But I blame you not. —Letter 5a, 1891.

Childish Behavior in Senior Workers

The eye of the Lord has been upon you. He has desired to open before you a way to do the work that you are capable of doing. Sister S, the Lord will give you the power of comprehending that in your own strength you cannot control yourself. You have the idea that everything must be done in *your way.* When you see others in active service, you are tempted to think that you are left out; and for this reason you easily become impatient.

The love of Christ must be an abiding principle in the soul. At your age, after your life of toil, can anything be more desirable than quietude, love, peace, restfulness, and time in which to prepare to meet your Lord in peace when He shall come? You are worn, and do not view things aright. To ask you to remain in the position of a trainer of the youth would be to bring upon you too great a burden. It would be a mistake to place you, with tired nerves, in a position full of perplexity. In the management of children you often manifest a species of severity.

Can there be any power so great as the power of love? Love to God and love to your neighbor—this is the whole duty that God requires of you. Do not spoil the good work that you have done. Withdraw from the turmoil of battle, and seek rest and peace in following God's way. Doors of usefulness will open to you. Brother S, take up the work that God has given you as an evangelist.

Brother and Sister S, the testing question now comes to you, Will you seek for rest and peace, cultivating all your powers for the future, immortal life? The Lord regards you with the greatest tenderness. Both of you need to have less responsibility in the school work. The Lord desires both of you to stand free from the burdens that you have hitherto carried. . . .

Neither of you is to feel as if you were divorced from the work. As it progresses, you should feel an interest in it, and be thankful that there are others who can carry it forward successfully. One laborer is adapted to one line of work, and another laborer to another line; all are to move forward together, advancing the work harmoniously. A Paul may plant, an Apollos water, but God gives the increase. The Lord uses some men to plow the field and to sow the seed, and others to reap; and He causes both those who sow and those who reap to rejoice together in the time of harvest. This is the way the Lord has always worked. He has given to every man his work. Let us do our best. If the Lord is with us, we shall be prospered. . . .

As you read this letter, I desire you to regard me as your best friend. I respect you both for your past faithfulness. You have a work to do for the Lord. But you are to bear less responsibility than you have borne in the past. The reason for my speaking especially of Sister S's being released from the work of teaching, is that she may have opportunity constantly to cultivate sweetness of disposition.

My sister, never cherish unhappy thoughts, or think that you are not treated right. You have become childish. You may not recognize this, nevertheless it is so. You need quietude and rest. You have strong likes and dislikes. Beware of hindering the work of God. Because I speak to you on these points, do not for a moment suppose that I wish to do you an injury.

My son Edson has labored untiringly to have both of you sustain the right relation to the school interest. Let God work out His infinite plans. Cooperate with Him as His helping hand in working out these plans. Stand not as hindrances, for thus you would cause things to be said and done that would hinder the work that you have called in wise helpers to advance.

My dear sister, I beseech you to put away all feelings of suspicion and jealousy. God's eye is over both of you. I am pained because I fear that this letter may possibly be misunderstood; but I am instructed to say to you, Know who your friends are, and appreciate them. When it is necessary for a work to be done in order to reform abuses that have crept into the church, thank the Lord that He has spoken. And when the Lord speaks to you, thank Him for saving you from future sorrow.

I am instructed to warn you to be careful what

manner of spirit you manifest in regard to enlarging and perfecting the school work, for you are not to suppose that, unaided, you are equal to the task of carrying forward the increasing work that you have begun. Create no dissension by unadvised words of criticism in regard to the course of others, even if some things which displease you may seem to have been unnecessarily done. It makes me sad to think that you have become discontented over trivial matters. —Letter 63, 1902.

Danger of Accepting Infidel Sentiments

Brother [G. C.] Tenney, you have been drawn away from the truth more than you have known, and your connection with men in Battle Creek has been to your great injury. The light of your past experience is going out.

I have been surprised and made sad to read some of your articles in the *Medical Missionary*, and especially those on the sanctuary question. These articles show that you have been departing from the faith. You have helped in confusing the understanding of our people. The correct understanding of the ministration in the heavenly sanctuary is the foundation of our faith.

If you had remained away from the seducing influences that Satan is exerting at the present time in Battle Creek, you might yet be standing on vantage ground.

We are very sorry to see the result of gathering a large number to Battle Creek. Ministers who have been believers in the foundation truths that have made us what we are—Seventh-day Adventists; ministers who went to Battle Creek to teach and uphold the truths of the Bible, are now, when old and gray-headed, turning from the grand truths of the Bible, and accepting infidel sentiments. This means that the next step will be a denial of a personal God, pulling down the bulwarks of the faith that are plainly revealed in the Scriptures. In the Word is given the warning, "Some shall depart from the faith, giving heed to seducing spirits, and doctrines of devils."—Letter 208, 1906.

Anxiety in Regard to Money

It is frequently the case that aged persons are unwilling to realize and acknowledge that their mental strength is failing. They shorten their days by taking care which belongs to their children. Satan often plays upon their imagination and leads them to feel a continual anxiety in regard to their money. It is their idol, and they hoard it with miserly care. They will sometimes deprive themselves of many of the comforts of life, and labor beyond their strength, rather than use the means which they have. In this way they place themselves in continual want, through fear that sometime in the future they shall want.

All these fears originate with Satan. He excites the organs which lead to slavish fears and jealousies which corrupt nobleness of soul and destroy elevated thoughts and feelings. Such persons are insane upon the subject of money. If they would take the position which God would have them, their last days might be their best and happiest. Those who have children in whose honesty and judicious management they have reason to confide, should let their children make them happy. Unless they do this, Satan will take advantage of their lack of mental strength and will manage for them. They should lay aside anxiety and burdens, and occupy their time as happily as they can, and be ripening up for heaven. — 1T 423, 424.

Money Cannot Ransom Your Soul

I regard you, my brother, as in great peril. Your treasure is laid up on the earth, and your heart is upon your treasure. But all the means you may accumulate, even though it should be millions, will not be sufficient to pay a ransom for your soul. Then do not remain in impenitence and unbelief, and in your case defeat the gracious purposes of God; do not force from His reluctant hand destruction of your property or affliction of your person.

How many there are who are now taking a course which must erelong lead to just such visitations of judgment. They live on day by day, week by week, year by year, for their own selfish interest. Their influence and means, accumulated through God-given skill and tact, are used upon themselves and their families without thought of their gracious Benefactor. Nothing is allowed to flow back to the Giver. Indeed, they come to regard life and its entrusted talents as their own; and if they render back to God that portion which He justly claims, they think that they have placed their Creator under obligation to them. At last His patience with these unfaithful stewards is exhausted; and He brings all their selfish, worldly schemes to an abrupt termination, showing them that as they have gathered for their own glory, He can scatter; and they are helpless to resist His power.

Brother J, I address you today as a prisoner of hope. But will you consider that your sun passed its meridian some time ago and is now rapidly declining? The evening has come. Do you not discern the lengthening shadows? You have but a little time left in which to work for yourself, for humanity, and for your Master. There is a special work to be done for your own soul if you are ever to be numbered with the overcomers.

How stands your life record? Is Jesus pleading in your behalf in vain? Shall He be disappointed in you? Some of your companions, who stood side by side with you, have already been summoned away. Eternity will reveal whether they were bankrupt in faith and failed to secure eternal life, or whether they were rich toward God and heirs of the "far more exceeding and eternal weight of glory." Will you not consider that the long forbearance of God toward you calls for repentance and humiliation of soul before Him?—5T 350, 351.

Place Affections on the Better Land

Our aged father T has his affections upon the things of this earth when they should be removed and he be ripening up for heaven. The life that he now lives he should live by faith in the Son of God; his affections should be on the better land. He should have less and less interest in the perishable treasures of earth, while eternal things, which are of the greatest consequence, should engage his whole interest. The days of his probation are nearly ended. Oh, how little time remains to devote to God! His energies are worn, his mind broken, and at best his services must be weak; yet if given heartily and fully, they are wholly acceptable. With your age, Brother T, has come an increase of selfishness and a more firm, earnest love for the treasures of this poor world.

Sister T loves this world. She is naturally selfish. She has suffered much with bodily infirmities. God permitted this affliction to come upon her, and yet would not permit Satan to take her life. God designed through the furnace of affliction to loosen her grasp upon earthly treasures. Through suffering alone could this be done. She is one of those whose systems have been poisoned by drugs. By taking these she has ignorantly made herself what she is; yet God did not suffer her life to be taken, but lengthened her years of probation and suffering that she might become sanctified through the truth, be purified, made white and tried, and, through the furnace of affliction, lose her dross, and become more precious than fine gold, even than the golden wedge of Ophir. — 2T 184.

STEWARDSHIP WHILE LIVING

The Work of Benevolence Twice Blessed

DIVINE wisdom has appointed, in the plan of salvation, the law of action and reaction, making the work of benevolence, in all its branches, twice blessed. God could have accomplished His object in saving sinners without the help of man, but He knew that man could not be happy without acting a part in the great work of redemption. That man might not lose the blessed results of benevolence, our Redeemer formed the plan of enlisting him as His co-worker. —RH March 23, 1897.

Would you make your property secure? Place it in the hand that bears the nailprint of the crucifixion. Retain it in your possession, and it will be to your eternal loss. Give it to God, and from that moment it bears His inscription. It is sealed with His immutability. Would you enjoy your substance? Then use it for the blessing of the suffering. —9T 50, 51.

In order to be happy ourselves, we must live to make others happy. It is well for us to yield our possessions, our talents, and our affections in grateful devotion to Christ, and in that way find happiness here and immortal glory hereafter. —3T 251.

Lay Up Treasures in Heaven

Christ entreats, "Lay up for yourselves treasures in heaven." This work of transferring your possessions to the world above is worthy of all your best energies. It is of the highest importance, and involves your eternal interests. That which you bestow in the cause of God is not lost. All that is given for the salvation of souls and the glory of God, is invested in the most successful enterprise in this life and in the life to come. Your talents of gold and silver, if given to the exchangers, are gaining continually in value, which will be registered to your account in the kingdom of heaven. You are to be the recipients of the eternal wealth that has increased in the hands of the exchangers. In giving to the work of God, you are laying up for yourselves treasures in heaven. All that you lay up above is secure from disaster and loss, and is increasing to an eternal, an enduring substance. —RH Jan. 24, 1888. (See also CS 342)

Stewardship a Personal Responsibility

Parents should exercise the right that God has given them. He entrusted to them the talents He would have them use to His glory. The children were not to become responsible for the talents of the father. While they have sound minds and good judgment, parents should, with prayerful consideration, and with the help of proper counselors who have experience in the truth and a knowledge of the divine will, make disposition of their property.

If they have children who are afflicted or are struggling in poverty, and who will make a judicious use of means, they should be considered. But if they have unbelieving children who have abundance of this world, and who are serving the world, they commit a sin against the Master who has made them His stewards, by placing means in their hands merely because they are their children. God's claims are not to be lightly regarded.

And it should be distinctly understood that because parents have made their will, this will not prevent them from giving means to the cause of God while they live. This they should do. They should have the satisfaction here, and the reward hereafter, of disposing of their surplus means while they live. They should do their part to advance the cause of God. They should use the means lent them by the Master to carry on the work which needs to be done in His vineyard.

The love of money lies at the root of nearly all the crimes committed in the world. Fathers who selfishly retain their means to enrich their children, and who do not see the wants of the cause of God and relieve them, make a terrible mistake. The children whom they think to bless with their means are cursed with it.

Money left to children frequently becomes a root of bitterness. They often quarrel over the property left them, and in case of a will, are seldom all satisfied with the disposition made by the father. And instead of the means left exciting gratitude and reverence for his memory, it creates dissatisfaction, murmuring, envy, and disrespect. Brothers and sisters who were at peace with one another are sometimes made at variance, and family dissensions are often the result of inherited means. Riches are desirable only as a means of supplying present wants, and of doing good to others. But inherited riches oftener become a snare to the possessor than a blessing. Parents should not seek to have their children encounter the temptations to which they expose them in leaving them means which they themselves have made no effort to earn.

I was shown that some children professing to believe the truth, would, in an indirect manner, influence the father to keep his means for his children, instead of appropriating it to the cause of God while he lives. Those who have influenced their father to shift his stewardship upon them, little know what they are doing. They are gathering upon themselves double responsibility, that of balancing the father's mind so that he did not fulfill the purpose of God in the disposition of the means lent him of God to be used to His glory, and the additional responsibility of becoming stewards of means that should have been put out to the exchangers by the father, that the Master could have received His own with usury.

Many parents make a great mistake in placing their property out of their hands into the hands of their children while they are themselves responsible for the use or abuse of the talents lent them of God. Neither parents nor children are made happier by this transfer of property. And the parents, if they live a few years even, generally regret this action on their part. Parental love in their children is not increased by this course. The children do not feel increased gratitude and obligation to their parents for their liberality. A curse seems to lie at the root of the matter, which only crops out in selfishness on the part of the children, and unhappiness and miserable feelings of cramped dependence on the part of the parents.

If parents, while they live, would assist their children to help themselves, it would be better than to leave them a large amount at death. Children who are left to rely principally upon their own exertions, make better men and women, and are better fitted for practical life, than those children who have depended upon their father's estate. The children left to depend upon their own resources generally prize their abilities, improve their privileges, and cultivate and direct their faculties to accomplish a purpose in life. They frequently develop characters of industry, frugality, and moral worth, which lie at the foundation of success in the Christian life. Those children for whom parents do the most, frequently feel under the least obligation toward them. —3T 121-123.

Shifting Responsibility to Others

Those Sabbathkeeping brethren who shift the responsibility of their stewardship into the hands of their wives, while they themselves are capable of managing the same, are unwise, and in the transfer displease God. The stewardship of the husband cannot be transferred to the wife. Yet this is sometimes attempted, to the great injury of both.

A believing husband has sometimes transferred his property to his unbelieving companion, hoping thereby to gratify her, disarm her opposition, and finally induce her to believe the truth. But this is no more nor less than an attempt to purchase peace, or to hire the wife to believe the truth. The means which God has lent to advance His cause the husband transfers to one who has no sympathy for the truth; what account will such a steward render when the great Master requires His own with usury?

Believing parents have frequently transferred their property to their unbelieving children, thus putting it out of their power to render to God the things that are His. By so doing, they lay off that responsibility which God has laid upon them, and place in the enemy's ranks means which God has entrusted to them to be returned to Him by being invested in His cause when He shall require it of them.

It is not in God's order that parents who are capable of managing their own business, should give up the control of their property, even to children who are of the same faith. These seldom possess as much devotion to the cause as they should, and they have not been schooled in adversity and affliction, so as to place a high estimate upon the eternal treasure, and less upon the earthly. The means placed in the hands of such is the greatest evil. It is a temptation to them to place their affections upon the earthly, and trust to property, and feel that they need but little besides. When means which they have not acquired by their own exertion, comes into their possession, they seldom use it wisely.

The husband who transfers his property to his wife, opens for her a wide door of temptation, whether she is a believer or an unbeliever. If she is a believer, and naturally penurious, inclined to selfishness and acquis-itiveness, the battle will be much harder for her with her husband's stewardship and her own to manage. In order to be saved, she must overcome all those peculiar, evil traits, and imitate the character of her divine Lord, seeking opportunity to do others good, loving others as Christ has loved us. She should cultivate the precious gift of love possessed so largely by our Saviour. His life was characterized by noble, disinterested benevolence. His whole life was not marred by one selfish act. — 1T 528, 529.

Dying Charity Versus Living Benevolence

I saw that many withhold from the cause while they live, quieting their consciences that they will be charitable at death; they hardly dare exercise faith and trust in God to give anything while living. But this deathbed charity is not what Christ requires of His followers; it cannot excuse the selfishness of the living. Those who hold fast their property till the last moment, surrender it to death rather than to the cause. Losses are occurring continually. Banks fail, and property is consumed in very many ways. Many purpose to do something, but they delay the matter, and Satan works to prevent the means from coming into the treasury at all. It is lost before it is returned to God, and Satan exults that it is so.

If you would do good with your means, do it at once lest Satan get it in his hands and thus hinder the work of God. Many times, when the Lord has opened the way for brethren to handle their means to advance His cause, the agents of Satan have presented some enterprise by which they were positive the brethren could double their means. They take the bait; their money is invested, and the cause, and frequently themselves, never receive a dollar.

Brethren, remember the cause; and when you have means at your command lay up for yourselves a good foundation against the time to come, that you may lay hold on eternal life. Jesus for your sakes became poor, that you through His poverty might be made rich in heavenly treasure. What will you give for Jesus, who has given all for you?

It will not do for you to depend on making your charity gifts in testamentary bequests at death. You cannot calculate with the least degree of surety that the cause will ever be benefited by them. Satan works with acute skill to stir up the relatives, and every false position is taken to gain to the world that which was solemnly dedicated to the cause of God. Much less than the sum willed is always received. Satan even puts it into the hearts of men and women to protest against their relatives' doing what they wish in the bestowment of their property. They seem to regard everything given to the Lord as robbing the relatives of the deceased. If you want your means to go to the cause, appropriate it, or all that you do not really need for a support, while you live. A few of the brethren are doing this and enjoying the pleasure of being their own executors. Will the covetousness of men make it necessary that they shall be deprived of life in order that the property which God has lent them shall not be useless forever? Let none of you draw upon yourselves the doom of the unprofitable servant who hid his Lord's money in the earth.

Dying charity is a poor substitute for living

benevolence. Many will to their friends and relatives all except a very small pittance of their property. This they leave for their supreme Friend, who became poor for their sakes, who suffered insult, mockery, and death, that they might become sons and daughters of God. And yet they expect when the righteous dead shall come forth to immortal life that this Friend will take them into His everlasting habitations.

The cause of Christ is robbed, not by a mere passing thought, not by an unpremeditated act. No. By your own deliberate act you made your will, placing your property at the disposal of unbelievers. After having robbed God during your lifetime, you continue to rob Him after your death, and you do this with the full consent of all your powers of mind, in a document called your will. What do you think will be your Master's will toward you for thus appropriating His goods? What will you say when an account is demanded of your stewardship?

Brethren, awake from your life of selfishness, and act like consistent Christians. The Lord requires you to economize your means and let every dollar not needed for your comfort flow into the treasury. Sisters, take that ten cents, that twenty cents, that dollar which you were about to spend for candies, for ruffles, or for ribbons, and donate it to God's cause. Many of our sisters earn good wages, but it is nearly all spent in gratifying their pride of dress.

The wants of the cause will continually increase as we near the close of time. Means is needed to give young men a short course of study in our schools, to prepare them for efficient work in the ministry and in different branches of the cause. We are not coming up to our privilege in this matter. All schools among us will soon be closed up. How much more might have been done had men obeyed the requirements of Christ in Christian beneficence! What an influence would this readiness to give all for Christ have had upon the world! It would have been one of the most convincing arguments in favor of the truth we profess to believe — an argument which the world could not misunderstand nor gainsay. . . .

Let us individually go to work to stimulate others by our example of disinterested benevolence. The work might have gone forward with far greater power had all done what they could to supply the treasury with means. —5T 154-157.

Business Affairs at Loose Ends?

Brother and Sister L should have confidence in the work for these last days, and should be perfecting Christian character, that they may receive the eternal reward when Jesus comes. Brother L is failing in physical and mental vigor. He is becoming incapable of bearing much responsibility. He should counsel with his brethren who are discreet and faithful.

Brother L is a steward of God. He has been intrusted with means, and should be awake to his duty, and render to God the things that are God's. He should not fail to understand the claims that God has upon him. While he lives, and has his reasoning powers, he should improve the opportunity of appropriating the property that God has intrusted to him, instead of leaving it for others to use and appropriate after the close of his life.

Satan is ever ready to take advantage of the weaknesses and infirmities of men to suit his own purposes. He is a wily adversary, and has outgeneraled many whose purposes were good to benefit the cause of God with their means. Some have neglected the work that God has given them to do in appropriating their means. And while they are negligent in securing to the cause of God the means that He has lent them, Satan comes in and turns that means into his own ranks.

Brother L should move more cautiously. Men who are not of our faith obtain means of him upon various pretenses. He trusts them, believing them to be honest. It will be impossible for him to get back all the means he has let slip out of his hands into the enemy's ranks. He could make a safe investment of his means by aiding the cause of God, and thus laying up for himself treasures in heaven. Frequently he is unable to help when he would, because he is crippled, and cannot command the means to do so. When the Lord calls for his means, it is frequently in the hands of those to whom he has lent it, some of whom never design to pay, and others feel no anxiety in the matter.

Satan will accomplish his purpose as thoroughly through dishonest borrowers as in any other way. All that the adversary of truth and righteousness is working for, is to prevent the advancement of our Redeemer's kingdom. He works through agents to carry out his purposes. If he can prevent means from going into the treasury of God, he is successful in one branch of his work. That means which should have been used to aid in the great plan of saving souls, he has retained in his ranks, to aid him in his work.

Brother L should have his business all straight, and not left at loose ends. It is his privilege to be rich in good works, and to lay up for himself a good foundation against the time to come, that he may lay hold on eternal life. It is not safe for him to follow his failing judgment. He should counsel with experienced brethren, and seek wisdom of God, that he may do up his work well. He should now be really in earnest, providing himself "bags which wax not old, a treasure in the heavens that faileth not."—2T 675, 676.

Help Needed Now

Many who are able to give liberally when the cause is in need, selfishly retain their means, and soothe their conscience with a plan for doing some great thing for the cause of God after their death. They make a will, giving a large sum to the church and its various interests, and then settle down with a feeling that they have done all that is required of them. Wherein have they denied self by this act? They have, on the contrary, revealed selfishness. When they have no further use for their money, they propose to give it to God. But they will retain it as long as they can, till they are compelled to relinquish it by a messenger that cannot be turned aside.

God has made us all His stewards, and in no case has He authorized us to neglect our duty or leave it for others to do. The call for means to advance the cause of truth will never be more urgent than now. Our money will never do a greater amount of good than at the present time. Every day of delay in rightly appropriating it is limiting the period in which it will do good in the saving of souls. If we leave others to accomplish that which God has left for us to do, we wrong ourselves and Him who gave us all we have. How can others do *our* work of benevolence any better than we can do it ourselves? So far as practicable, God would have every man an executor of his own will in this matter, during his lifetime.

Adversity, accident, or intrigue may cut off forever intended acts of benevolence, when he who has accumulated a fortune is no longer by to guard it. It is sad that so many neglect the golden opportunity to do good in the present, but wait to be cast out of their stewardship before giving back to the Lord the means which He has lent them to be used for His glory.

One marked feature in the teachings of Christ is the frequency and earnestness with which He rebuked the sin of covetousness, and pointed out the danger of worldly acquisitions and the inordinate love of gain. In the mansions of the rich, in the temple, and in the streets, He warned those who inquired after salvation: "Take heed, and beware of covetousness." "Ye cannot serve God and mammon."

It is this increasing devotion to money-getting, the selfishness which the desire for gain begets, that deadens the spirituality of many in the church, and removes from them the favor of God. When the head and hands are constantly occupied with planning and toiling for the accumulation of riches, the claims of God and humanity are forgotten.

If God has blessed us with prosperity, it is not that our time and attention should be diverted from Him and given to that which He has lent us. The giver is greater than the gift. We have been bought with a price; we are not our own. Have we forgotten that infinite price paid for our redemption? Is gratitude dead in the heart? Does not the cross of Christ put to shame a life of selfish ease and indulgence?—RH Nov. 15, 1906.

New Fields That Must Be Worked

Dear Brother Craw:

I write you because you and I are getting old, and we need now to carefully examine ourselves. What are we doing with the talent of means lent us by the Master? What have you done during your life, my brother? Have you returned to the Lord that which is truly His? Do you feel that you have done all He requires of you to advance His work? While praying over the matter of our great need of money with which to enter new fields and lift up the standard in places where the truth has never been preached, you were presented to me. It was as though your name was spoken, and the Lord said, "He has My entrusted money, and it would be for his own eternal interest to place it in new missionary fields that must be worked."

I decided to write to you, my brother. Cannot you send us a donation in our great need? If the Lord signifies to you that He wants the money you have to be used in the advancement of His work, will you not send me money to invest? I have used everything of my own, and now I ask you to return to the Lord His own entrusted goods. We see so many fields opening in every direction. People are calling for us to come and hold meetings with them, and we dare not refuse. I have tried to mortgage my place, but the banks in Australia do not care to invest money in this way. The Lord has indicated plainly that you could relieve us by investing means in the good work. There is a great work to be done, and we wish to move in the opening providence of God. Considerable advancement has been made, and we cannot stop now.

I address you definitely. Will you now give back a portion of your Lord's money, and relieve us in our pressing necessity? May the Lord make your heart willing, is my prayer. We wish to do everything that it is possible to do to save souls from perishing in their sins. One soul is of more value than the whole world. We realize that a good work is being done. About thirty-five souls have been baptized in Newcastle, and fifteen more are waiting for baptism. The whole place is aroused. The cities near Newcastle must be worked. Shall we be hindered for lack of money when it is in the hands of God's stewards and should come to us?

In the parable we are shown that every one has received something from the Master. Each is to do his part in supplying the needs that occur in advancing the truth. Property is a talent. The Lord sends His message: "Sell that ye have, and give alms." All that we have is the Lord's, without any question. "The silver is Mine and the gold is Mine," saith the Lord of hosts. Why should we not, when pressed financially, present our great need to those whom God has signified hold His money in trust, to be used in advancing the work of saving souls ready to perish? We do not want you to sow sparingly, because then you will reap sparingly. We want you, my brother, to lay up treasure in heaven. They that sow bountifully shall reap also bountifully. The reaping will be proportionate to the sowing. Read the ninth chapter of Second Corinthians.

Soon Christ will reward every man according to his works. Soon your money will pass out of your hands for another to handle. It will then not be the test of your stewardship. Now it is yours, by which the Lord desires to try you. While you are alive, be your own almoner and receive the blessings that will come to you in a faithful discharge of duty. Give back to God that which is His own. This is God's way. He always lends His talents to His stewards, to be used to spread the knowledge of the truth. This work cannot be done without the funds that are in the hands of God's servants.

We now invite you to dispose of your property. This the Lord calls upon you to do. We have to build meetinghouses and hospitals for our sick. We want means to advance the work of God in this new world. Be liberal, that God may advance His cause. —Letter 53, 1899.

God Will Teach Us Our Duty

There are poor men and women who are writing to me for advice as to whether they shall sell their homes, and give the proceeds to the cause. They say the appeals for means stir their souls, and they want to do something for the Master who has done everything for them. I would say to such, "It may not be your duty to sell your little homes just now; but go to God for yourselves; the Lord will certainly hear your earnest prayers for wisdom to understand your duty." If there was more seeking God for heavenly wisdom, and less seeking wisdom from men, there would be far greater light from Heaven, and God would bless the humble seeker.

But I can say to those to whom God has intrusted goods, who have lands and houses: "Commence your selling, and giving alms. Make no delay. God expects more of you than you have been willing to do." We call upon you who have means, to inquire with earnest prayer: What is the extent of the divine claim upon me and my property? There is work to be done now to make ready a people to stand in the day of the Lord. Means must be invested in the work of saving souls who, in turn, shall bring their offerings to the treasury, and win souls to the Lord. —RH Extra, Dec. 11, 1888.

IMPORTANCE OF WILLS

Executors of the Saviour's Will

CHRIST loves the human race, and in every action of His life He has expressed this love. He calls upon men to love one another as He has loved them. His saving power and love are ever to be the theme of those who believe in God.

Just before His ascension, He gave to His disciples the commission: "Go ye therefore, and teach all nations, baptizing them in the name of the Father, and of the Son, and of the Holy Ghost: teaching them to observe all things whatsoever I have commanded you: and, lo, I am with you alway, even unto the end of the world."

Thus was given to the disciples a most precious trust. They were to be the executors of the will in which Christ has bequeathed to the world the treasure of eternal life. They realized the responsibility of their work. They knew that they held in their hands the bread of life for a famishing world, and they went everywhere preaching the word. The love of Christ constrained them, and they could not forbear breaking the bread of life to all who were in need. The last words of the Saviour were constantly sounding in their ears.

In the trust given to the first disciples, each believer has a share. Each one is to be an executor of the Saviour's will. Each one has been given sacred truth to give to the earnest seeker. Every believer is to be a laborer together with God. —RH Jan. 7, 1902.

Not to Be Postponed

To the aged, who are losing their hold on this life, I appeal to make a right disposition of your Lord's goods before you fall asleep in Jesus. Remember that you are God's stewards. Give back to the Lord His own while you live. Do not fail of attending to this while you have your reason. As age comes upon us, it is our duty to make a disposition of our means to the instrumentalities that God has established. Satan is using every device to divert from the Lord's cause the means so much needed. Many are binding up their talent of means in worldly enterprises, when the cause of God needs every dollar to advance His truth and glorify His name. I ask: Shall we not lay up for ourselves treasure in heaven, in bags that wax not old?

I would especially urge the aged who are soon to make a disposal of their means to remember those who have ministered faithfully in word and doctrine. Place your means where, should health and life fail, they can be invested in the cause of God. Thus they will be put out to the exchangers and be constantly accumulating. —7T 295, 296.

When Satan Controls Business Matters

God is displeased with the slack, loose manner in which many of His professed people conduct their worldly business. They seem to have lost all sense of the fact that the property they are using belongs to God, and that they must render to Him an account of their stewardship. Some leave their worldly business in perfect confusion. Satan has his eye on it all, and he strikes at a favorable opportunity, and by his management takes much means out of the ranks of Sabbath keepers. And this means goes into his ranks.

Some who are aged are unwilling to make any set-tlement of their worldly business, and in an unexpected moment they sicken and die. Their children who have no interest in the truth, take the property. Satan has managed it as suited him. "If therefore ye have not been faithful in the unrighteous mammon, who will commit to your trust the true riches? And if ye have not been faithful in that which is another man's, who shall give you that which is your own?"

I was shown the awful fact that Satan and his angels have had more to do with the management of the property of God's professed people than the Lord has. Stewards of the last days are unwise. They suffer Satan to control their business matters, and get into his ranks what belongs to, and should be in, the cause of God. God takes notice of you, unfaithful stewards; He will call you to account.

I saw that the stewards of God can by faithful, judicious management keep their business in this world square, exact, and straight. And it is especially the privilege and duty of the aged, the feeble, and those who have no children, to place their means where it can be used in the cause of God if they should be suddenly taken away. But I saw that Satan and his angels exult over their success in this matter. And those who should be wise heirs of salvation almost willingly let their Lord's money slip out of their hands into the enemy's ranks. In this way they strengthen Satan's kingdom, and seem to feel very easy about it! — 1T 199, 200.

When Legal Advice Is Important

At the camp meeting in Vermont, in 1870, I felt urged by the Spirit of God to bear a plain testimony relative to the duty of aged and wealthy parents in the disposition of their property. I had been shown that some men who are shrewd, prudent, and sharp in regard to the transaction of business generally, men who are distinguished for promptness and thoroughness, manifest a want of foresight and promptness in regard to a proper disposal of their property while they are living. They know not how soon their probation may close; yet they pass on from year to year with their business unsettled, and frequently their lives finally close without their having the use of their reason. Or they may die suddenly, without a moment's warning, and their property be disposed of in a manner that they would not have approved. These are guilty of negligence; they are unfaithful stewards.

Christians who believe the present truth should manifest wisdom and foresight. They should not neglect the disposition of their means, expecting a favorable opportunity to adjust their business during a long illness. They should have their business in such a shape that, were they called at any hour to leave it, and should they have no voice in its arrangement, it might be settled as they would have had it were they alive. Many families have been dishonestly robbed of all their property, and have been subjected to poverty, because the work that might have been well done in an hour had been neglected. Those who make their wills should not spare pains or expense to obtain legal advice, and to have them drawn up in a manner to stand the test.

I saw that those who profess to believe the truth should show their faith by their works. They should, with the unrighteous mammon, make friends, that they may finally be received into everlasting habitations. God has made men stewards of means. He has placed in their hands the money with which to carry forward the great work for the salvation of souls for whom Christ left His home, His riches, His glory, and became poor that He might, by His own humiliation and sacrifice, bring many sons and daughters of Adam to God. In His providence, the Lord has ordained that the work in His vineyard should be sustained by the means intrusted to the hands of His stewards. A neglect on their part to answer the calls of the cause of God in carrying forward His work, shows them to be unfaithful and slothful servants. —3T 116, 117.

Wills Should Stand Test of Law

Some wills are made in so loose a manner that they will not stand the test of the law, and thus thousands of dollars have been lost to the cause. Our brethren should feel that a responsibility rests upon them, as faithful servants in the cause of God, to exercise their intellect in regard to this matter, and secure to the Lord His own.

Many manifest a needless delicacy on this point. They feel that they are stepping upon forbidden ground when they introduce the subject of property to the aged or to invalids in order to learn what disposition they design to make of it. But this duty is just as sacred as the duty to preach the word to save souls. Here is a man with God's money or property in his hands. He is about to change his stewardship. Will he place the means which God has lent him to be used in His cause, in the hands of wicked men, just because they are his relatives? Should not Christian men feel interested and anxious for that man's future good as well as for the interest of God's cause, that he shall make a right disposition of his Lord's money, the talents lent him for wise improvement? Will his brethren stand by, and see him losing his hold on this life, and at the same time robbing the treasury of God? This would be a fearful loss to himself and to the cause, for, by placing his talent of means in the hands of those who have no regard for the truth of God, he would, to all intents and purposes, be wrapping it in a napkin and hiding it in the earth.

The Lord would have His followers dispense their means while they can do it themselves. Some may inquire, "Must we actually dispossess ourselves of everything which we call our own?" We may not be required to do this now, but we must be willing to do so for Christ's sake. We must acknowledge that our possessions are absolutely His, by using of them freely whenever means is needed to advance His cause. Some close their ears to the calls made for money to be used in sending missionaries to foreign countries, and in publishing the truth and scattering it like autumn leaves all over the world.

Such excuse their covetousness by informing you that they have made arrangements to be charitable at death. They have considered the cause of God in their wills. Therefore they live a life of avarice, robbing God in tithes and in offerings, and in their wills return to God but a small portion of that which He has lent them, while a very large proportion is appropriated to relatives who have no interest in the truth. This is the worst kind of robbery. They rob God of His just dues, not only all through life, but also at death.

It is utter folly to defer to make a preparation for the future life until nearly the last hour of the present life. It is also a great mistake to defer to answer the claims of God for liberality to His cause until the time comes when you are to shift your stewardship upon others. Those to whom you entrust your talents of means may not do as well with them as you have done. How dare rich men run so great risks? Those who wait till death before they make a disposition of their property, surrender it to death rather than to God. In so doing, many are acting directly contrary to the plan of God plainly stated in His Word. If they would do good, they must seize the present golden moments, and labor with all their might, as if fearful that they may lose the favorable opportunity.

Those who neglect known duty by not answering to God's claims upon them in this life, and who soothe their consciences by calculating on making their bequests at death, will receive no words of commendation from the Master, nor will they receive a reward. They practiced no self-denial, but selfishly retained their means as long as they could, yielding it up only when death claimed them.

That which many propose to defer until they are about to die, if they were Christians indeed they would do while they have a strong hold on life. They would devote themselves and their property to God, and, while acting as His stewards, they would have the satisfaction of doing their duty. By becoming their own executors, they could meet the claims of God themselves, instead of shifting the responsibility upon others.

We should regard ourselves as stewards of the Lord's property, and God as the supreme proprietor, to whom we are to render His own when He shall require it. When He shall come to receive His own with usury, the covetous will see that instead of multiplying the talents entrusted to them, they have brought upon themselves the doom pronounced upon the unprofitable servant.

The Lord designs that the death of His servants shall be regarded as a loss, because of the influence for good which they exerted and the many willing offerings which they bestowed to replenish the treasury of God. Dying legacies are a miserable substitute for living benevolence. The servants of God should be making their wills every day, in good works and liberal offerings to God. They should not allow the amount given to God to be disproportionately small when compared with that appropriated to their own use. In making their wills daily, they will remember those objects and friends that hold the largest place in their affections.

Their best friend is Jesus. He did not withhold His

own life from them, but for their sakes became poor, that through His poverty they might be made rich. He deserves the whole heart, the property, all that they have and are. But many professed Christians put off the claims of Jesus in life, and insult Him by giving Him a mere pittance at death.

Let all of this class remember that this robbery of God is not an impulsive action, but a well-considered plan which they preface by saying, "Being in sound mind." After having defrauded the cause of God through life, they perpetuate the fraud after death. And this is with the full consent of all the powers of the mind. Such a will many are content to cherish for a dying pillow. Their will is a part of their preparation for death, and is prepared so that their possessions shall not disturb their dying hours. Can these dwell with pleasure upon the requirement that will be made of them to give an account of their stewardship?

We must all be rich in good works in this life, if we would secure the future, immortal life. When the judgment shall sit, and the books shall be opened, every man will be rewarded according to his works. Many names are enrolled on the church book that have robbery recorded against them in the ledger of heaven. And unless these repent, and work for the Master with disinterested benevolence, they will certainly share in the doom of the unfaithful steward.

It often happens that an active businessman is cut down without a moment's warning, and on examination his business is found to be in a most perplexing condition. In the effort to settle his estate, the lawyers' fees eat up a large share, if not all, of the property, while his wife and children and the cause of Christ are robbed. Those who are faithful stewards of the Lord's means will know just how their business stands, and, like wise men, they will be prepared for any emergency. Should their probation close suddenly, they would not leave such great perplexity upon those who are called to settle their estate.

Many are not exercised upon the subject of making their wills while they are in apparent health. But this precaution should be taken by our brethren. They should know their financial standing, and should not allow their business to become entangled. They should arrange their property in such a manner that they may leave it at any time.

Wills should be made in a manner to stand the test of law. After they are drawn, they may remain for years, and do no harm, if donations continue to be made from time to time as the cause has need. Death will not come one day sooner, brethren, because you have made your will. In disposing of your property by will to your relatives, be sure that you do not forget God's cause. You are His agents, holding His property; and His claims should have your first consideration. Your wife and children, of course, should not be left destitute; provision should be made for them if they are needy. But do not, simply because it is customary, bring into your will a long line of relatives who are not needy.

Let it ever be kept in mind that the present selfish system of disposing of property is not God's plan, but man's device. Christians should be reformers, and break up this present system, giving an entirely new aspect to the formation of wills. Let the idea be ever present that it is the Lord's property which you are handling. The will of God in this matter is law.

If man had made you the executor of his property, would you not closely study the will of the testator, that the smallest amount might not be misapplied? Your heavenly Friend has entrusted you with property, and given you His will as to how it should be used. If this will is studied with an unselfish heart, that which belongs to God will not be misapplied. The Lord's cause has been shamefully neglected, when He has provided men with sufficient means to meet every emergency, if they only had grateful, obedient hearts.

Those who make their wills should not feel that when this is done they have no further duty, but they should be constantly at work using the talents entrusted to them, for the upbuilding of the Lord's cause. God has devised plans that all may work intelligently in the distribution of their means. He does not propose to sustain His work by miracles. He has a few faithful stewards, who are economizing and using their means to advance His cause. Instead of self-denial and benevolence being an exception, they should be the rule. The growing necessities of the cause of God require means. Calls are constantly coming in from men in our own and foreign countries for messengers to come to them with light and truth. This will necessitate more laborers and more means to support them. — 4T 479-483.

REMARRIAGE
IN OLD AGE

Counsel to Joseph Hare, Sr.

DEAR Brother Hare: I will say in regard to your received in the mail before the last, I have no special light upon this subject and cannot give you information upon the point that interests you. I advise you to consult with Wesley Hare and his wife, as they know the one you have in mind and would be the proper counselors. I know, as you say, that you must be lonely in your old age, and if there is one whom you could love, and who would reciprocate that love, I see no objection. But as I do not know the lady you have in mind, I cannot speak as could one who knows both parties.

One thing is certain: You know that He whom you have served for many years will be to you a safe Counselor. Rest your case with Him who never makes a mistake. Our time now, both yours and mine, is short, and we need to be ripening for the future immortal life. Christ says, "Let not your heart be troubled: ye believe in God, believe also in Me. In My Father's house are many mansions: if it were not so, I would have told you. I go to prepare a place for you. And if I go and prepare a place for you, I will come again, and receive you unto Myself; that where I am, there ye may be also" [John 14:1-3]. Let us rejoice in this, and take on just as few worries as possible.

The invitation to old and young is, "Come unto

Me, all ye that labor and are heavy laden, and I will give you rest. Take My yoke upon you, and learn of Me; for I am meek and lowly in heart; and ye shall find rest unto your souls" [Matt. 11:28-30]. Thank the Lord, with heart and soul and voice, that there is a haven of rest, sweet rest. It is your privilege, and it is my privilege, to accept the invitation, and rest. We want now that our remnant of life should be as free as possible from every perplexity and care, that we shall have repose in the life of Christ. "My yoke," He says, "is easy, and My burden is light."

The Lord will not disappoint any who put their trust in Him. He will be first and last and best in everything to us. He will be a present help in every time of need. In these last days of service we shall . . . be held, and led, and protected, by the power of Christ. May the Lord bless and strengthen you, that your last days may be your best days, fragrant with the softening, subduing influence of His love. The Lord bless and keep you and give you repose in His love, is my most earnest desire for you, my brother. —TSB 31-33 (Letter 70, 1898).

Advice to J. N. Andrews

I advised you to marry before you returned the last time to Europe for these reasons. First, you needed a wife to care for you and [you] should not have taken your family to Europe without a good companion to be a mother to your children, that these children might not in all things bear the stamp of your mind and be molded according to your ideas. Your mind is not equally balanced. You need another element brought into your labors that you do not possess and that you do not understand is really essential. . . .

Your ideas have been erroneous to preserve your life as a widower, but on this point I will say no more. The influence of a noble Christian woman of proper capabilities would have served to counteract the tendencies of your mind. The ability of concentrativeness, the intense light in which you view everything of a religious character connected with the cause and work of God, has brought upon you depression of spirits, a weight of anxiety that has weakened you physically and mentally. If you had been connected with one who would have opposite feelings, who would have ability to turn your thoughts away from gloomy subjects, who would not have yielded her individuality, but have preserved her identity and had a molding influence upon your mind, you would today have had physical strength and power to resist disease. —TSB 34.

You remember I wrote you from Texas to obtain a wife before you returned to Europe. Do you suppose I would have given you such advice if I had no light upon the matter? Be assured, no such counsel would have been given you without good reason. I was shown [that] you follow your own judgment and your own ideas altogether too tenaciously. If you were more willing to be counseled by those you should confide in, and trust less to your own feelings and impressions, the result for yourself and for the cause of God would be far better.

I was shown that you made a mistake in starting to

Europe without a companion. If you had, before starting, selected you a godly woman who could have been a mother to your children, you would have done a wise thing, and your usefulness would have been tenfold to what it has been. —TSB 34, 35.

Remarriage of S. N. Haskell*

We received Brother Haskell's letter the evening after the Sabbath. We were glad to hear from you that your interests are united as one. May the Lord bless this union, that you may be a strength and support to one another at all times. May the peace of God rest upon you, is my sincere desire and earnest prayer. "Go, stand and speak . . . to the people all the words of this life" [Acts 5:20].

I am pleased, Brother Haskell, that you have a helper [Mrs. Haskell]. This is that which I have desired for some time. The work in which we are engaged has made us one in Christ Jesus to diffuse the knowledge of Jesus Christ. It is your privilege to have happiness in your new relation to each other, in ministering the gospel to those who are in darkness and error. We can sympathize and unite in the grand work that you and I love, and which is the one great object ever before us—the enlargement of the kingdom of Christ and the celebration of His glory. In everything which relates to this we are united in bonds of Christian fellowship, in companionship with heavenly intelligences. . . .

Because of the light given me, I am fully possessed

* Elder Haskell's first wife died in 1894. In 1897, when he remarried, he was 64 and his new wife, Hettie Hurd, was 40.

with the conviction that through your united agencies, as sanctified instrumentalities, light shall be reflected to the salvation of many souls that are now in darkness and error. I know you have not lived unto yourselves but unto Him whom you love and whom you serve and worship. — TSB 33, 34.

George I. Butler's Desire to Remarry*

May, 1902

Dear Brother and Sister Keck:

My mind has been burdened during the night season. I have learned that Brother Butler has thought of marrying Sister Keck's sister. Some of the brethren, in talking with me about this matter, expressed their disapproval, saying that they thought that such a step would hurt Brother Butler's influence, especially should he marry so soon after his wife's death. At the time I gave the subject scarcely a thought, but in the night season I was talking with one in regard to the matter, and the subject assumed a different aspect.

Then I seemed to be talking with someone else, of whom I was asking the question, "Why do you regard this attachment as so objectionable?" The answer was, "He is so much older than she is." "But," I said, "would it be proper or wise for him to marry a woman of his own age? What help could such a woman be to him in his ministry? At his age, Elder Butler should have the care that only a wife can give. If this young woman has a

---

* Elder Butler's first wife died November 18, 1901, leaving him a widower at the age of 67. Even though he had Ellen White's approval, opposition from Mrs. Keck and from Hiland Butler, Elder Butler's son, kept him from going forward with his intention to marry Mrs. Keck's sister in 1902. In 1907, at the age of 73, he finally married again.

desire to give him this care, why should anyone forbid her? She is, I understand, about thirty-five years old."

Sister Haskell married Elder Haskell because she was convinced that he needed a helper in his work. The difference in their ages seemed to Elder Haskell to be a barrier against their union. He asked my opinion and advice. I said, "If her mind is drawn out in this direction, do not hesitate. You need the help of a spiritual-minded, intelligent woman, who can sustain and encourage you in your work." They were married, and the Lord has greatly blessed their union, making their lives doubly useful to His cause and work.

May it not be possible that the hand of the Lord is in this attachment between Elder Butler and Sister Keck's sister? What others may think in regard to this matter is not to find any place in our reckoning. We are to ask, "Is this union the will of the Lord?" May it not be His plan for the increase of the helpfulness and usefulness of each?

For many years, because of his invalid wife, Elder Butler has been shut away from the work, cut off from many privileges, prevented from doing the work he might have done. He has cared faithfully and tenderly for his wife, who was weak in mind and body, hampered by affliction and infirmity. When she died, he buried her in sorrow, yet not as a man who is without hope.

After his wife's death, he began to plan for his sister, who has been living with him for a few years, to visit her friends, as she had desired. But the Lord saw fit to add another sorrow to his life. Very suddenly and unexpectedly Sister Lockwood [Elder Butler's sister] died.

Elder Butler is a man who needs the softening influence of a good, high-principled woman. The companionship of such a woman would indeed be a great blessing to him. Considering his experience for the last fifteen years, is it strange that he desires a younger person than himself to love, to converse with?

You do not reason altogether correctly. Saith the Lord, "My thoughts are not your thoughts, neither are your ways My ways. . . . For as the heavens are higher than the earth, so are My ways higher than your ways, and My thoughts than your thoughts." The Lord surprises us by His manner of dealing.

Elder Butler is strong in physical and spiritual health. The Lord has proved and tested and tried him, as He did Job, and as He did Moses. I see in Elder Butler one who has humbled his soul before God. He has another spirit than the Elder Butler of younger years. He has been learning his lesson at the feet of Jesus. After caring so long for his suffering, afflicted wife, he has come forth from the furnace fire refined and purified. I respect and love my brother as one of God's servants.

I have no more to say, except that if your sister, being a Christian, is led and taught by God, leave her with God. Do not by human wisdom spoil the Lord's plan and hinder His work. Elder Butler needs the help of a strong, kind, intelligent woman, who can cooperate with him in his sphere of usefulness, encouraging him and holding up his hands, aiding him to do a good and acceptable work for the Master. If your sister is that woman, she may feel honored in uniting with Elder Butler.

At first I thought that such a step would hurt Brother Butler's influence. But I have had time to consider the matter, and I now see it in another light. I came to this decision before I had the pleasure of meeting Elder Butler at the time of his visit to my home.

I wish you to understand that I have not had one word of conversation with Elder Butler in regard to this matter. He has not made the slightest reference to it. —Letter 77, 1902.

May 23, 1902

Dear Brother and Sister Keck:

I wish to add a few lines to the letter I have already written you. We had a very profitable visit with Elder Butler. He left us last Wednesday morning for Healdsburg. W. C. White and his wife rode over with him in the carriage. . . .

My brother and sister, I wish you to take to the Lord the matter of the union of your sister with Elder Butler. Prayerfully consider your objections; and then, in the light of the words I have written, if your sister is disposed to unite with Elder Butler in marriage, see if you cannot give up your objection, for the reason that this union may be the purpose of God.

I see in Elder Butler a man of usefulness, a man of intelligence and Bible study. His ministry would be much more valuable were he united with a woman who could help him in his work. Think of how much more he could accomplish with the help of a discreet, intelligent woman. He should not be left to live alone and to travel alone. The sooner he can find a good wife, the better it will be for his work. A wife could do for him those things that no male companion could do—look after his clothes, see that they are free from dust, and that he is always prepared to appear before large congregations.

Would it not be best for you to withdraw your opposition to this union? It is not best for you in any way to oppose that which the Lord may have ordained. It may be that the Lord sees that by this union your sister and Elder Butler could accomplish more for Him than they otherwise could. What people may say has nothing to do with this matter. If it is the Lord's purpose, let us not be found fighting against Him. —Letter 78, 1902.

Unwise Counsel From a Son

I beg of you not to reproach your father. You should not feel as you do, for your father has done nothing that God condemns. His condemnation exists only in the minds of men. He has in no wise dishonored his children. He is keeping the way of the Lord, to do justice and judgment. The Lord is opening the way before him, that he may do a great and good work for His people. Christ is his Saviour, and in beholding Christ he will be changed into His image.

Your father has been a kind, tender husband. For many years he served faithfully her whom he has always loved. Death separated him from the one who for so long has been his special charge. Then his sister was taken from him, and his home was broken up. Is it any wonder that under these circumstances he should, after your mother's death, become attached to a woman in whose conversion to the truth he was instrumental? This woman is not young, but of an age to be a help to him in his work. Should your father's age have stood as a barrier to his happiness? . . .

Had your father married this lady, I believe that the Lord would greatly have blessed them both. But I do not think, seeing that the matter has been treated as it has, it will go any further. Those who refused to sanction this union should remember that one day they must meet the result of their action. But I must leave this matter with those who have been acting a part in it. — TSB 35, 36 (written July 28, 1902, to Hiland Butler, George I. Butler's son).

Ellen White Chose Not to Remarry

Since twenty-one years ago when I was deprived of my husband by death, I have not had the slightest idea of ever marrying again. Why? Not because God forbade it. No. But to stand alone was the best for me, that no one should suffer with me in carrying forward my work entrusted to me of God. And no one should have a right to influence me in any way in reference to my responsibility and my work in bearing my testimony of encouragement and reproof.

My husband never stood in my way to do this, although I had help and encouragement from him, and oft his pity. His sympathy and prayers and tears I have missed so much, so very much. No one can understand this as myself. But my work has to be done. No human power should give the least supposition that I would be influenced in the work God has given me to do in bearing my testimony to those for whom He has given me reproof or encouragement.

I have been alone in this matter, severely alone, with all the difficulties and all the trials connected with the work. God alone could help me. The last work that is to be done by me in this world will soon be finished. I must express myself plainly, in a manner, if possible, not to be misunderstood. —Ms 227, 1902.

When Ages Widely Differ

Another cause of the deficiency of the present generation in physical strength and moral worth, is, men and women uniting in marriage whose ages widely differ. It is frequently the case that old men choose to marry young wives. By thus doing, the life of the husband has often been prolonged, while the wife has had to feel the want of that vitality which she has imparted to her aged husband. It has not been the duty of any woman to sacrifice life and health, even if she did love one so much older than herself, and felt willing on her part to make such a sacrifice. She should have restrained her affections. She had considerations higher than her own interest to consult. She should consider, if children be born to them, what would be their condition? It is still worse for young men to marry women considerably older than themselves. The offspring of such unions in many cases, where ages widely differ, have not well-balanced minds. They have been deficient also in physical strength. In such families have frequently been manifested varied, peculiar, and often painful, traits of character. They often die prematurely, and those who reach maturity, in many cases, are deficient in physical and mental strength, and moral worth.

The father is seldom prepared, with his failing faculties, to properly bring up his young family. — 2SM 423, 424.

CONSERVING LIFE'S ENERGIES

Short Discourses, Longer Life

MY dear brother [George I. Butler]:

We shall have trials. But I am instructed to say to you and to others, that laborers often bring upon themselves greater taxation than is required. The counsel given is, Cut the discourses short. Were a long discourse divided, and only one-half given, it would be better retained in the minds of the hearers than the whole of a long discourse. This counsel belongs to me as well as to you. Except when I have a special message to bear, I am determined to speak briefly because it is best.

I am growing old, but I do not feel the weight of years. I have always been afflicted, ever since I was nine years old. And at seventy-eight I suffer less pain than I suffered in my earlier years. But I am now determined to take care of my strength, and I shall not weary others by long talking. I want you, as one of the old hands and the experienced workers, to live to be able to bear your testimony, as did John [the Revelator].

We are personally under the training of God. Let us trust in God, for we need His help constantly. You do too much talking at one time, and so do I. It is not best to put this extra strain upon ourselves that is unnecessary. We need to hold more testimony meetings. Please consider the words I bear to you. Save your strength. I am afraid for so old a man to bear such heavy burdens. We do want you to have a clear testimony to bear just at this period of the earth's history. We want you to have a clear mind, that you may counsel together with those of like precious faith.

Let us do our best to bring about unity. I am in a position where I cannot change the past experience if I would; for the Lord has led me and has given me such evidence of His power in every advance movement of our work, that I have assurance, made doubly sure, as [to] every position we now hold as truth. We cannot distrust such manifestations of the Lord's power in defining what is truth. I am charged that we are to hold the beginning of our confidence firm unto the end. We now need clearly to define what is truth, and let not the enemy steal a march on us.

We know, and Elder Haskell and Elder Loughborough know also, of the earlier history of this work. There are few now alive who passed through the experience of 1843 and 1844. Let us be careful of our life power. Do not work too hard. —Letter 88, 1906.

When Sleep Will Not Come, Pray

June 23, 1892. Another night has passed. I slept only three hours. I was not in so much pain as usual, but was restless and nervous. After lying awake for some time, trying to sleep, I gave up the effort, and directed my whole attention to seeking the Lord. How precious to me was the promise, "Ask, and it shall be given you; seek, and ye shall find; knock, and it shall be opened unto you" (Matt. 7:7). I prayed most earnestly to the Lord for comfort and peace, which the Lord Jesus alone can give. I want the blessing of the Lord, so that, while suffering pain, I shall not lose self-control. I dare not trust in self for one moment. —2SM 235.

A Rest Period in the Daytime

Dear Brother [S. N.] Haskell:*

I urge you not to work above that which you are able to do. You should have less constant, taxing labor, that you may be able to keep yourself in a rested condition. You should take a sleep in the daytime. You can then think more readily, and your thoughts will be more clear and your words more convincing. And be sure to bring your whole being into connection with God. Accept the Holy Spirit for your spiritual illumination, and under its guidance follow on to know the Lord. Go forth where the Lord directs, doing what He commands. Wait on the Lord, and He will renew your strength.

But it is not required of you or of me to be on a continual strain. We should surrender continually what He requires of us, and He will show us His covenant. "The secret of the Lord is with them that fear Him" (Ps. 25:14). We shall be instructed more deeply in the mystery of God the Father and of Jesus Christ. We shall have visions of the King in His beauty, and before us will be opened the rest that remaineth for the people of God. We will soon enter the city whose builder and maker is God—the city we have long talked of. —2SM 230, 231.

---

* Elder Haskell was 73 and Ellen White was 79 when this letter was written.

Adequate Diet and Rest

Dear Brother Bates:*

I have been informed that you have taken but one meal a day for a period of time; but I know it to be wrong in your case, for I have been shown that you needed a nutritious diet, and that you were in danger of being too abstemious. Your strength would not admit of your severe discipline.

You should not carry the burden of leading the church in meetings. Younger hands should do this, and you should not bear the responsibility. You should not feel that you are required to hold meetings yourself, having the charge in different places, for your mind and your physical strength are not equal to the task. You are in danger of heaping responsibilities upon you and feeling that the Lord requires it of you, after He has released you from active, physical taxation. You should gracefully and honorably lay the burden down, and seek for quiet rest, fitting up for your last change. You feel much tried and grieved if your Advent brethren do not look to you to lead, when I have been shown it is wrong for them to let the leading of the church rest on you.

I think that you have erred in fasting two days. God did not require it of you. I beg of you to be cautious and eat freely good, wholesome food twice a day. You will surely decrease in strength and your mind become unbalanced unless you change your course of abstemious diet.

I have advised Brother Charles Jones not to encour-

---

* Written to Joseph Bates in the last year of his life. He died at the age of eighty.

age or allow you to go into different churches to labor. You are not in a condition of body and mind to labor. You must stop and rest and be happy, and not worry your mind about the responsibilities of the work and cause of God. Be peaceful, calm, and happy, and trust yourself in the work and cause of God, feeling that you are now to soften, sweeten, ripen up for heaven. God loves you. But, with your advanced age and your strong peculiarities, you will certainly mar the work of God more than you can help it.

You have simply to rest in the hands of God and feel that your work to preach the truth is done. Have no further responsibility in this direction. You can be free to bear your testimony to comfort yourself; this is your privilege; but to bear any church labor in word or doctrine, or to travel out among other churches to hold public meetings, God has released you.—Letter 2, 1872.

Overstrained Ideas of Health Reform

Poor, half-decayed fruit and vegetables should never be placed upon the table because it is a savings of a few pennies. This kind of management is a loss, and the body that should be nourished as a temple of the Holy Ghost and be fitted to do the very best kind of work is neglected. Many speeches were made in regard to self-denial and self-sacrifice that were wholly inappropriate and uncalled for.

Brother M was so reduced by poor food and by want of conveniences and proper, careful attention while absent from his family, that he had no strength to withstand exposure and disease. He died a martyr to misconceived, crooked ideas of what constitutes health reform and self-denial. He always had little thought for his own convenience, and was left too much to himself, to care for himself. He was willing to do anything to save means. Such conscientious souls are the ones who are hurt by these overstrained ideas of what constitutes health reform.

Sister R's family have been injured by the ideas she has entertained of health reform. Brother John has been a hard worker, and the food taken into his stomach has not nourished him; it has not supplied the waste of his system and has not made the best quality of blood. The weakness from which he is now suffering is caused by a poverty of the blood more than by any real disease.

Why will not men and women to whom God has given reasoning powers exercise their reason? When they see their strength is failing, why do they not investigate their habits and their diet, and change to a different diet to see its effect? The sufferings that have been brought about by a so-called health reform have militated greatly against true reforms. These narrow ideas and this overstraining in the diet question have done great injury to physical, mental, and moral strength.

Our missions should be conducted in a merciful way. It never pays to cheat the stomach of healthful, wholesome food; for it is robbing the blood of nourishment, and in consequence the whole system is deranged, the whole mind diseased, and God has lame, inefficient service in place of healthy, sound labor. . . . There are sufferers on every hand because people do not think that the body needs special favors. —Letter 12, 1887.

Faithful in Health Reform*

The question of how to preserve the health is one of primary importance. When we study this question in the fear of God we shall learn that it is best, for both our physical and our spiritual advancement, to observe simplicity in diet. Let us patiently study this question. We need knowledge and judgment in order to move wisely in this matter. Nature's laws are not to be resisted, but obeyed.

Those who have received instruction regarding the evils of the use of flesh foods, tea and coffee, and rich and unhealthful food preparations, and who are determined to make a covenant with God by sacrifice, will not continue to indulge their appetite for food that they know to be unhealthful. God demands that the appetites be cleansed, and that self-denial be practiced in regard to those things which are not good. This is a work that will have to be done before His people can stand before Him a perfected people. . . .

There are some professed believers who accept certain portions of the Testimonies as the message of God, while they reject those portions that condemn their favorite indulgences. Such persons are working contrary to their own welfare and the welfare of the church. It is essential that we walk in the light while we have the light. Those who claim to believe in health reform, and yet work counter to its principles in the daily life prac-

---

* Portion of manuscript read to the delegates at the 1909 General Conference session.

tice, are hurting their own souls and are leaving wrong impressions upon the minds of believers and unbelievers. — 9T 153, 154.

Healthful Building Locations

So far as possible, all buildings intended for human habitation should be placed on high, well-drained ground. This will ensure a dry site. . . . This matter is often too lightly regarded. Continuous ill health, serious diseases, and many deaths result from the dampness and malaria of low-lying, ill-drained situations.

In the building of houses it is especially important to secure thorough ventilation and plenty of sunlight. Let there be a current of air and an abundance of light in every room in the house. Sleeping rooms should be so arranged as to have a free circulation of air day and night. No room is fit to be occupied as a sleeping room unless it can be thrown open daily to the air and sunshine. In most countries bedrooms need to be supplied with conveniences for heating, that they may be thoroughly warmed and dried in cold or wet weather.

The guestchamber should have equal care with the rooms intended for constant use. Like the other bedrooms, it should have air and sunshine and should be provided with some means of heating to dry out the dampness that always accumulates in a room not in constant use. Whoever sleeps in a sunless room or occupies a bed that has not been thoroughly dried and aired does so at the risk of health, and often of life. . . .

Those who have the aged to provide for should remember that these especially need warm, comfortable rooms. Vigor declines as years advance, leaving less vitality with which to resist unhealthful influences; hence the greater necessity for the aged to have plenty of sunlight and fresh, pure air. —AH 148, 149.

A Prescription for Healing

When the gospel is received in its purity and power, it is a cure for the maladies that originated in sin. The Sun of Righteousness arises, "with healing in His wings" (Mal. 4:2). Not all that this world bestows can heal a broken heart, or impart peace of mind, or remove care, or banish disease. Fame, genius, talent—all are powerless to gladden the sorrowful heart or to restore the wasted life. The life of God in the soul is man's only hope.

The love which Christ diffuses through the whole being is a vitalizing power. Every vital part—the brain, the heart, the nerves—it touches with healing. By it the highest energies of the being are roused to activity. It frees the soul from the guilt and sorrow, the anxiety and care, that crush the life forces. With it come serenity and composure. It implants in the soul, joy that nothing earthly can destroy—joy in the Holy Spirit—health-giving, life-giving, joy.

Our Saviour's words, "Come unto Me, . . . and I will give you rest" (Matt. 11:28), are a prescription for the healing of physical, mental, and spiritual ills. Though men have brought suffering upon themselves by their own wrongdoing, He regards them with pity. In Him they may find help. He will do great things for those who trust in Him. —MH 115.

Jesus was the fountain of healing mercy for the world; and through all those secluded years at Nazareth, His life flowed out in currents of sympathy and tenderness. The aged, the sorrowing, and the sin-burdened, the children at play in their innocent joy, the little creatures of the groves, the patient beasts of burden—all were happier for His presence. —DA 74.

The Importance of Exercise

Inactivity is the greatest curse that could come upon most invalids. Light employment in useful labor, while it does not tax mind or body, has a happy influence upon both. It strengthens the muscles, improves the circulation, and gives the invalid the satisfaction of knowing that he is not wholly useless in this busy world. He may be able to do but little at first, but he will soon find his strength increasing, and the amount of work done can be increased accordingly.

Exercise aids the dyspeptic by giving the digestive organs a healthy tone. To engage in severe study or violent physical exercise immediately after eating, hinders the work of digestion; but a short walk after a meal, with the head erect and the shoulders back, is a great benefit.

Notwithstanding all that is said and written concerning its importance, there are still many who neglect physical exercise. Some grow corpulent because the system is clogged; others become thin and feeble because their vital powers are exhausted in disposing of an excess of food. The liver is burdened in its effort to cleanse the blood of impurities, and illness is the result.

Those whose habits are sedentary should, when the weather will permit, exercise in the open air every day, summer or winter. Walking is preferable to riding or driving, for it brings more of the muscles into exercise. The lungs are forced into healthy action, since it is impossible to walk briskly without inflating them.

Such exercise would in many cases be better for the health than medicine. —MH 240.

No Exercise Can Take the Place of Walking

Those who are feeble and indolent should not yield to their inclination to be inactive, thus depriving themselves of air and sunlight, but should practice exercising out of doors in walking or working in the garden. They will become very much fatigued, but this will not injure them. You, my sister, will experience weariness, yet it will not hurt you; your rest will be sweeter after it. Inaction weakens the organs that are not exercised. And when these organs are used, pain and weariness are experienced, because the muscles have become feeble. It is not good policy to give up the use of certain muscles because pain is felt when they are exercised. The pain is frequently caused by the effort of nature to give life and vigor to those parts that have become partially lifeless through inaction. The motion of these long-disused muscles will cause pain, because nature is awakening them to life.

Walking, in all cases where it is possible, is the best remedy for diseased bodies, because in this exercise all the organs of the body are brought into use. Many who depend upon the movement cure could accomplish more for themselves by muscular exercise than the movements can do for them. In some cases want of exercise causes the bowels and muscles to become enfeebled and shrunken, and these organs that have become enfeebled for want of use will be strengthened by exercise. There is no exercise that can take the place of walking. By it the circulation of the blood is greatly improved. —3T 78.

FORTITUDE
IN AFFLICTION*

During Prolonged Illness

EVERY mail has taken from one to two hundred pages from my hand, and most of it has been written either as I am now propped up on the bed by pillows, half lying or half sitting, or bolstered up sitting in an uncomfortable chair.

It is very painful to my hip and to the lower part of my spine to sit up. If such easy chairs were to be found in this country [Australia] as you have at the sanitarium, one would be readily purchased by me, if it cost thirty dollars. . . . It is with great weariness that I can sit erect and hold up my head. I must rest it against the back of the chair on the pillows, half reclining. This is my condition just now.

But I am not at all discouraged. I feel that I am sustained daily. In the long weary hours of the night, when sleep has been out of the question, I have devoted much time to prayer; and when every nerve seemed to be shrieking with pain, when if I considered myself, it seemed I should go frantic, the peace of Christ has come into my heart in such measure that I have been filled with gratitude and thanksgiving. I know that Jesus loves me, and I love Jesus. Some nights I have slept three hours, a few nights four hours, and much of the

---

* Late in 1891, Ellen G. White, in response to a request from the General Conference, journeyed to Australia to assist in strengthening the newly established work there. The sojourn extended to nine years. Soon after her arrival she was overtaken by an extended and painful illness. The citations in this section record her fortitude in this affliction. See 2SM 233-242.

time only two, and yet in these long Australian nights, in the darkness, all seems light about me, and I enjoy sweet communion with God.

When I first found myself in a state of helplessness I deeply regretted having crossed the broad waters. Why was I not in America? Why at such expense was I in this country? Time and again I could have buried my face in the bed quilts and had a good cry. But I did not long indulge in the luxury of tears.

I said to myself, "Ellen G. White, what do you mean? Have you not come to Australia because you felt that it was your duty to go where the conference judged it best for you to go? Has this not been your practice?"

I said, "Yes."

"Then why do you feel almost forsaken and discouraged? Is not this the enemy's work?"

I said, "I believe it is."

I dried my tears as quickly as possible and said, "It is enough; I will not look on the dark side any more. Live or die, I commit the keeping of my soul to Him who died for me."

I then believed that the Lord would do all things well, and during this eight months of helplessness, I have not had any despondency or doubt. I now look at this matter as a part of the Lord's great plan, for the good of His people here in this country, and for those in America, and for my good. I cannot explain why or how, but I believe it. And I am happy in my affliction. I can trust my heavenly Father. I will not doubt His love. I have an ever-watchful guardian day and night, and I will praise the Lord, for His praise is upon my lips because it comes from a heart full of gratitude. — Letter 18a, 1892.

Prayer and Anointing— but Not Instantly Healed

May 21, 1892. The trying, almost sleepless night is ended. Yesterday afternoon Elder [A. G.] Daniells and his wife, Elder [G. C.] Tenney and his wife, and Brethren Stockton and Smith came to our house at my request to pray that the Lord would heal me. We had a most earnest season of prayer, and we were all much blessed. I was relieved, but not restored. I have now done all that I can to follow the Bible directions, and I shall wait for the Lord to work, believing that in His own good time He will heal me. My faith takes hold of the promise, "Ask, and ye shall receive" (John 16:24).

I believe that the Lord heard our prayers. I hoped that my captivity might be turned immediately, and to my finite judgment it seemed that thus God would be glorified. I was much blessed during our season of prayer, and I shall hold fast to the assurance then given me: "I am your Redeemer; I will heal you."—Ms 19, 1892.

Jesus Knows Our Griefs and Pains

June 26, 1892. I am glad when the daylight comes, for the nights are long and wearisome. But when I cannot sleep, gratitude fills my heart as I think that One who never slumbers is watching over me for good.

What a wonderful thought it is that Jesus knows all about the pains and griefs we bear. In all our afflictions He was afflicted. Some among our friends know nothing of human woe or physical pain. They are never sick, and therefore they cannot enter fully into the feelings of those who are sick. But Jesus is touched with the feeling of our infirmity. He is the great medical missionary. He has taken humanity upon Himself, and has placed Himself at the head of a new dispensation, in order that He may reconcile justice and compassion.—Ms 19, 1892.

"Make Me a Healthy, Fruit-bearing Branch"

June 29, 1892. My prayer on awaking is, Jesus, keep Thy child today. Take me under Thy guardianship. Make me a healthy, fruit-bearing branch of the living Vine. "Without Me," Christ says, "ye can do nothing" (John 15:5). In and through Christ we can do all things.

He who was the adored of angels, who had listened to the music of the heavenly choir, was ever touched, while upon this earth, with the sorrows of children, ever ready to listen to the story of their childish woe. He often dried their tears, cheering them with the tender sympathy of His words, which seemed to hush their sorrows and make them forget their grief. The emblem in the form of a dove that hovered over Jesus at His baptism represents His gentleness of character.—Ms 19, 1892.

"Let No Unkind Words
Be Spoken by Me"

June 30, 1892. Another night of great weariness is nearly passed. Although I continue to suffer much pain, I know that I am not forsaken by my Saviour. My prayer is, Help me, Jesus, that I may not dishonor Thee with my lips. Let no unkind words be spoken by me. —Ms 19, 1892.

"I Will Not Complain"

July 6, 1892. I am so thankful that I can tell the Lord all my fears and perplexities. I feel that I am under the shield of His wings. An infidel once asked a God-fearing youth, "How great is the God you worship?" "So great," was the reply, "that He fills immensity, and yet so small that He dwells in every sanctified heart."

O precious Saviour, I long for Thy salvation. "As the hart panteth after the water brooks, so panteth my soul after Thee" (Ps. 42:1). I long for a clearer view of Jesus. I love to think of His spotless life, to meditate upon His lessons. How many times I repeat the words, "Come unto Me, all ye that labor and are heavy laden, and I will give you rest" (Matt. 11:28).

Much of the time my body is full of pain, but I will not by complaining become unworthy of the name of Christian. I am assured that this lesson of suffering will be to the glory of God, a means of warning others to avoid continuous labor under trying circumstances so unfavorable to health of the body. —Ms 19, 1892.

"The Lord Strengthens Me"

July 7, 1892. The Lord strengthens me by His grace to write important letters. The brethren frequently come to me for counsel. I feel a strong assurance that this tedious affliction is for the glory of the Lord. I will not murmur; for when I wake in the night, it seems that Jesus is looking upon me. The fifty-first chapter of Isaiah is exceedingly precious to me. He bears all our burdens. I read this chapter with assurance and hope. —Ms 19, 1892.

No Thought of Beating a Retreat

July 10, 1892. I awoke Emily* at five o'clock to build my fire and help me to dress. I thank the Lord that I had a better night's rest than usual. My wakeful hours I employ in prayer and meditation. The question forces itself upon me, Why do I not receive the blessing of restoration to health? Shall I interpret these long months of sickness as evidences of the displeasure of God because I came to Australia? I answer decidedly, No, I dare not do this. At times before leaving America I thought that the Lord did not require me to go to a country so far away, at my age and when I was prostrated by overwork. But I followed the voice of the [General] Conference, as I have ever tried to do at times when I had no clear light myself. I came to Australia, and found the believers here in a condition where they must have help. For weeks after reaching here I labored as earnestly as I have ever labored in my life. Words

---

* Emily Campbell, Mrs. White's traveling companion and secretary.

were given me to speak in regard to the necessity of personal piety. . . .

I am in Australia, and I believe that I am just where the Lord wants me to be. Because suffering is my portion, I have no thought of beating a retreat. The blessed assurance is given me that Jesus is mine and that I am His child. The darkness is dispelled by the bright beams of the Sun of Righteousness. Who can understand the pain I suffer but the One who is afflicted in all our afflictions? To whom can I speak but to Him who is touched with the feeling of our infirmities, and who knows how to succor those who are tempted?

When I pray earnestly for restoration, and it seems that the Lord does not answer, my spirit almost faints within me. Then it is that the dear Saviour makes me mindful of His presence. He says to me, Cannot you trust Him who has purchased you with His own blood? I have graven thee on the palms of My hands. Then my soul is nourished with the divine Presence. I am lifted out of myself, as it were, into the presence of God. —Ms 19, 1892.

God Knows What Is Best

July 14, 1892. When the affliction under which I have been suffering for several months came upon me, I was surprised that it was not removed at once in answer to prayer. But the promise, "My grace is sufficient" (2 Cor. 12:9), has been fulfilled in my case. There can be no doubt on my part. My hours of pain have been hours of prayer, for I have known to whom to take my sorrows. I have the privilege of reinforcing my feeble strength by laying hold upon infinite power. By day and night I stand on the solid rock of God's promises.

My heart goes out to Jesus in loving trust. He knows what is best for me. My nights would be lonely did I not claim the promise, "Call upon Me in the day of trouble: I will deliver thee, and thou shalt glorify Me" (Ps. 50:15). —Ms 19, 1892.

Lessons From the Months of Suffering

I have been passing through great trial in pain and suffering and helplessness, but through it all I have obtained a precious experience more valuable to me than gold. When I was first convinced that I must give up my cherished plans to visit the churches in Australia and New Zealand, I felt to seriously question whether it was my duty to leave America and come to this far-off country. My sufferings were acute. Many sleepless hours of the nights I spent in going over and over our experience since we left Europe for America, and it has been a continual scene of anxiety, suffering, and burden bearing. Then I said, What does it all mean?

I carefully reviewed the history of the past few years and the work the Lord gave me to do. Not once did He fail me, and often He manifested Himself to me in a marked manner, and I saw I had nothing of which to complain, but instead precious things running like threads of gold through all my experience. The Lord understood better than I the things that I needed, and I felt that He was drawing me very nigh to Himself, and I must be careful not to dictate to God as to what He should do with me. This unreconciliation was at the beginning of my sufferings and helplessness, but it was not long until I felt that my affliction was a part of God's plan. I found that by partly lying and partly sitting I could place myself in position to use my crippled hands, and although suffering much pain I could do considerable writing. Since coming to this country I have written sixteen hundred pages of paper of this size.

Many nights during the past nine months I was enabled to sleep but two hours a night, and then at times darkness would gather about me; but I prayed, and realized much sweet comfort in drawing nigh to God. The promises, "Draw nigh to God, and He will draw nigh to you" (James 4:8), "When the enemy shall come in like a flood, the Spirit of the Lord shall lift up a standard against him" (Isa. 59:19), were fulfilled to me. I was all light in the Lord. Jesus was sacredly near, and I found the grace given sufficient, for my soul was stayed upon God, and I was full of grateful praise to Him who loved me and gave Himself for me. I could say from a full heart, "I know whom I have believed" (2 Tim. 1:12). "God is faithful, who will not suffer you to be tempted above that ye are able; but will with the temptation also make a way to escape, that ye may be able to bear it" (1 Cor. 10:13). Through Jesus Christ I have come off more than conqueror, and held the vantage ground.

I cannot read the purpose of God in my affliction, but He knows what is best, and I will commit my soul, body, and spirit to Him as unto my faithful Creator. "For I know whom I have believed, and am persuaded that He is able to keep that which I have committed unto Him against that day" (2 Tim. 1:12). —Letter 7, 1892.

Expect Short-Term Memory Problems

He who has grown old in the service of God may find his mind a blank in regard to the things that are happening about him, and recent transactions may soon pass from his memory; but his mind is all awake to the scenes and transactions of his childhood. —SD 78.

Rest in His Love

We honor God and our Lord Jesus Christ when we rest in His love. You are one of the Lord's witnesses, whom He will never leave nor forsake. I am instructed to say to you, He has pardoned all your sins, and put upon you the white robe of His righteousness. All He requires of you now is to rest in His love. He has you in His keeping. You have fought the battles of the Lord Jesus Christ, you have kept the faith, and henceforth there is laid up for you a crown of life, to be your reward in that day when life and immortality shall be given to all who have kept the faith and have not denied the Saviour's name.

That your mind is clouded is no evidence that Christ is not your precious Saviour. Now that the childhood of age has come upon you, He regards you as no less His child. Your religious life bears its testimony now as in the past. You have believed the word of God, and in perplexities and trials have acted according to that word. Like the apostle you may say, "I have fought a good fight, I have finished my course, I have kept the faith: henceforth there is laid up for me a crown of righteousness, which the Lord, the righteous judge, shall give me at that day: and not to me only, but unto all them also that love His appearing" (2 Tim. 4:7, 8). —Letter 299, 1904.

ASSURANCE AND COMFORT FOR THOSE FACING DEATH

Messages of Sympathy and Hope to a Faithful Assistant*

Melrose, Massachusetts
August 17, 1904

DEAR Sister Marian Davis:

I would be pleased to be at home, but just what meetings I shall consent to attend is uncertain; therefore we will do the very best we can. . . .

I am asking the Lord to strengthen you. We are hopeful that you are better. Do keep fast hold of the Lord, your hand in the hand of Christ. . . .

Marian, you must not become discouraged. Your case is in the hands of the Lord, and you must now submit your case in regard to treatment to let the physicians, Dr. A and Dr. B, do those things for you that must be done. We have other books to put in your hands when you shall overcome the illness now upon you. Be sure to eat, even if it causes some pain. The longer you refrain from eating, the weaker you will become. . . . We may inquire, How can the Lord have need of us? Is not our God full of might? Will you not lay hold on His strength? No living being can help you as the Lord Jesus can. Trust in Him. He

---

* Marian Davis, who joined Mrs. White's staff in 1879 and was associated with her in the work in America, Europe, and Australia for twenty-five years, contracted tuberculosis in 1903, and a year later closed her lifework. Miss Davis was a faithful and trusted literary assistant, much beloved by Mrs. White. See 2SM 251-254.

will care for you. —Letter 378, 1904.

Melrose, Massachusetts
August 24, 1904

Dear Sister Marian Davis:

Let not one anxious thought come into your mind. I am sorry you are so ill, but do everything you can on your part for the recovery of your health. I will see that all bills of expense shall be settled. I am not well; not able to travel but a little distance in the carriage. I dare not commit myself to the lengthy journeys on the cars. As long as you and I shall live, my home is your home. . . .

Marian, nearly the whole time I have been away I have not relished food, but I dare not cease to eat, for then I could do nothing. I have eaten when I could not relish food, in order that I might live. I have relished food since I came to this place. I put my trust in God and plead with Him for you and for myself. We are to have no anxieties or cares. Just put your trust in the Lord. All that is needed for you and me is to believe and trust in Him who is able to save to the uttermost all who come unto Him and will put their trust in Him. "Hold fast My hand," Jesus says to you and me. You are encouraged to think right thoughts upon Christ our Saviour—your Saviour and my Saviour. You have rejoiced in every opportunity of doing what you could to promote His glory, and you will be led into the city of God when the last trump of God shall sound, and we shall be received with genuine joy.

Marian, you have been united with me to bring

sound doctrine into actual contact with human souls, that they may catch the inspiration and produce sound practice. "The form of sound words" is to be prized above gold and silver and every earthly attraction. You have loved the truth. You have felt intensely over the great neglect our Lord and Saviour has been receiving. Oh, to be like-minded with God! This you have longed for. There is no genuine saving elevation for man apart from the truth of God.

"Bless the Lord, O my soul: and all that is within me, bless His holy name" (Ps. 103:1). Now please let you and me have a thanksgiving service every day. Is it not due Him who has spared your life these many years in answer to the prayer of faith? Give yourself into His hands in your weakness, and trust in Him fully. We will take the Word of God as the grand rule of our lives, the heavenly panacea in our hand. We have tried, you and I united, to bring before minds the true form of doctrine, mingling holiness, mercy, truth, and love. We have tried to present these in simplicity, so that souls shall grasp mingled love and holiness—which is simply Christianity in the heart. We have done what we could do to present Christianity as the crown and glory of man's life here in this world, preparatory to entrance into the city of God to be His dear, precious redeemed ones in the mansions He has gone to prepare for us. Then praise the Lord. Let us praise Him.

Please eat, Marian, because your earthly physician would have you eat, and the great Medical Missionary would have you eat; and Sister [M. J.] Nelson will get anything you ask for. No one can be more pleased than

I to have your life spared to continue to do the work; but if your or my time is come to fall asleep in Jesus, we must not shorten life by refusing the nourishment that the system must have. Now eat, my dear, whether you want to eat or not, and thus act your part toward recovery. Do your very best to recover, and then if it please the Lord to give you rest, you have done what you could. I appreciate your labors. Praise the Lord, Marian, that Jesus, the Great Physician, can heal you. In love. —Letter 379, 1904.

College View, Nebraska
September 16, 1904

Dear Sister Marian:

I keep your case before me, and I am grieved that you are troubled in mind. I would comfort you if it were in my power. Has not Jesus, the precious Saviour, been to you so many times a present help in times of need? Do not grieve the Holy Spirit, but cease worrying. This is what you have many times talked to others. Let the words of those who are not sick, as you are, comfort you, and may the Lord help you, is my prayer.

If it is the Lord's will that you should die, you should feel that it is your privilege to commit your whole being, body, soul, and spirit, into the hands of a just and merciful God. He has no such feelings of condemnation as you imagine. I want you to stop thinking that the Lord does not love you. Cast yourself unreservedly upon the merciful provisions that He has made. He is waiting for you to heed His invitation. . . . You need not think that you have done anything which would lead God to treat you with severity. I know better. Just believe in His love, and take Him at His word. . . . No suspicion or distrust is to take possession of our minds. No apprehension of the greatness of God is to confuse our faith.

May God help us to humble ourselves in meekness and lowliness. Christ laid aside His royal robe and kingly crown, that He might associate with humanity, and show that human beings may be perfect. Clad in the garments of mercy He lived in our world a perfect life, to give us evidence of His love. He has done that which should make unbelief in Him impossible. From His high command in the heavenly courts He stooped to take human nature upon Him. His life is an example of what our lives may be. That no apprehension of God's greatness should come in to efface our belief in God's love, Christ became a man of sorrows and acquainted with grief. The human heart, given up to Him, will become a sacred harp, sending forth sacred music. —Letter 365, 1904.

College View, Nebraska
September 26, 1904

Dear Sister Marian:

We pray your life may be preserved until we meet you once more—but you may not die, but live. . . .

Look to Jesus. Trust in Jesus, whether you live or

die. He is your Redeemer. He is our Life-giver. If you fall asleep in Jesus He will bring you forth from the grave to a glorious immortality. May He give you peace and comfort and hope and joy from henceforth.

Put your entire trust in Jesus. He will never leave you nor forsake you. He says, I have graven you upon the palms of My hands. Marian, if you go before I do, we shall know each other *there.* We shall see as we are seen and know as we are known. Just let the peace of Christ come into your soul. Be true in your trust because He is true to His promise. Lay your poor, nervous hand in His firm hand and let Him hold you and strengthen you, cheer and comfort you. I will now get ready to leave this place. Oh, I wish I were with you this moment! In much love. —Letter 382, 1904.

Comfort to a Minister Dying of Cancer

We do not forget you; we remember you in our prayers at the family altar. I lie awake nights pleading with God in your behalf.

Oh, I feel so sorry for you. I will continue to pray that the blessing of God may rest upon you. He will not leave you comfortless. This world is of but little account, but, my dear brother and sister, Jesus says, "Ask, and it shall be given you; seek, and ye shall find; knock, and it shall be opened unto you" (Matt. 7:7). I plead this promise in your behalf. . . .

My brother, one night I seemed to be leaning over you, and saying: "Only a little longer, only a few more pangs of pain, a few more suffering hours, and then rest, blessed rest. In a special manner you will find peace. All humanity must be tested and tried. All of us must drink the cup and be baptized with affliction. But Christ has tasted death for every man in its bitterest form. He knows how to pity, how to sympathize. Only rest in His arms; He loves you, and He has redeemed you with His everlasting love. Be thou faithful unto death, and thou shalt receive a crown of life.

"All who live in our world from henceforth will know the meaning of trials. I know that God will give you grace, that He will not forsake you. Call to mind the promise of God: 'Write, Blessed are the dead which die in the Lord from henceforth: Yea, saith the Spirit, that they may rest from their labours; and their works do follow them' (Rev. 14:13). Be of good courage. I would be with you now if I could, but we shall meet in the morning of the resurrection.". . .

I was also speaking words of comfort to Sister C. I was encouraging her, and the room seemed to be filled with angels of God. Let both of you be of good courage. The Lord will not leave nor forsake you. — 2SM 256.

Deeds Preserved Through Eternal Ages

God's messengers are to hold aloft the standard of truth until the hand is palsied in death. When they sleep in death, the places that once knew them know them no more. The churches in which they preached, the places they visited to hold forth the word of life, still remain. The mountains, the hills, the things seen by mortal vision, are still there. All these things must at last pass away. The time is coming when the earth shall reel to and fro and shall be removed like a cottage. But the thoughts, the purposes, the acts of God's workers, although now unseen, will appear at the great day of final retribution and reward. Things now forgotten will then appear as witnesses, either to approve or to condemn.

Love, courtesy, self-sacrifice—these are never lost. When God's chosen ones are changed from mortality to immortality, their words and deeds of goodness will be made manifest, and will be preserved through the eternal ages. No act of unselfish service, however small or simple, is ever lost. Through the merits of Christ's imputed righteousness, the fragrance of such words and deeds is forever preserved. —RH March 10, 1904.

Christ Will Lead Us Safely Home

Was ever an instance known where a dying Christian gave to his watching friends the testimony that he had been deceived, that there is no God, no reality in the religion of Christ? But how many of those who have drawn about them the dark robes of atheism have let them fall before the grim messenger of death. We might cite many instances where learned men have gloried in their unbelief, and in parading their atheism. But when death claimed them, they have looked with horror into the starless future, and their dying words have been, "I have tried to believe that there is no God, no reward for the faithful, no punishment for the wicked. But how vain has been the attempt. I know now that I must meet the doom of the lost."

Sir Thomas Scott in his last moments cried: "Until this moment I believed there was neither a God nor a hell. Now I know and feel that there are both, and that I am doomed to perdition by the just judgment of God."

Voltaire was at one time the lion of the hour. He lived in a splendid mansion, and was surrounded by every luxury that heart could wish. Kings honored him. The great men of the world sought his society. On one occasion men took his horses from his carriage, and drew him themselves in triumph around the city. . . .

Go now to the death-bed of a Christian—Halburton of Scotland. He was in poverty, and was suffering great pain. He had none of the comforts that Voltaire possessed, but he was infinitely richer. He said: "I shall shortly die. In the resurrection I shall come forth to see my God and to live forevermore. I bless His name that I have found Him, and I die rejoicing in Him. I bless God that I was ever born."

Giving an account of the last days of Sir Davis Brewster, his daughter writes: "He thanked God that the way of salvation was so simple. No labored argument, no hard attainment, was required. To believe in the Lord Jesus Christ was to live. He trusted in Him, and enjoyed His peace." The last words of this great man of science were: "Life has been very bright to me, and now there is the brightness beyond. I shall see Jesus, who created all things, who made the worlds. I shall see Him as He is. Yes, I have had the Light for many years. Oh, how bright it is! I feel so safe, so satisfied."

"The way of the transgressor is hard," but wisdom's "ways are ways of pleasantness, and all her paths are peace." In the downward road the gateway may be bright with flowers, but there are thorns in the path. The light of hope which shines from its entrance fades into the darkness of despair; and the soul who follows that path descends into the shadows of unending night.

But he who takes Christ for his guide will be led safely home. The road may be rough, and the ascent steep; there may be pitfalls upon the right hand and upon the left; we may have to endure toil in our journey; when weary, when longing for rest, we may have to toil on; when faint, we may have to fight; when discouraged, we must still hope; but with Christ as our guide, we shall not fail of reaching the desired haven at last. Christ has trodden the rough way before us, and has smoothed the path for our feet.

Those who walk in wisdom's ways are, even in tribulation, exceedingly joyful, for He whom their soul loveth walks invisible beside them. At each upward step they discern more distinctly the touch of His hand; at every step, brighter gleamings of glory from the Unseen fall upon their path; and their songs of praise, reaching ever a higher note, ascend to join the songs of the angels before the throne. "The path of the righteous is as the light of dawn, that shineth more and more unto the perfect day."—ST Aug. 3, 1904.

The Grave Consecrated by Christ

Christ has consecrated the grave by passing through death. The Lord Jesus broke the fetters of the tomb, and proclaimed over the rent sepulcher of Joseph, "I am the resurrection, and the life" (John 11:25). The grave is consecrated by His presence. Footsteps of Him that bore the cross are traceable in His life and testify of His character. —Letter 103, 1898.

Our Washing and Ironing Time

We know in whom we believe. Men may talk about our having our minds fixed too much upon heaven, but we know better. We have been in the work nearly forty-eight years, and we know something about God's service. I know best what bereavement is when I stand here alone, when he who stood by my side, and on whose large affections I have leaned for thirty years, is gone, and yet I am not alone, for Christ is my helper. Oh, I wish the curtains could be rolled back and we could see Christ in His glory. We are to be members of the royal family, children of the heavenly King. Now it is our privilege to know that Christ is by our side as our helper.

Christ says, "I know thy works." He knows whether you are living a life of perfection and if you love to talk and think of Him, and whether it is your joy to praise Him. Do we expect to get to heaven at last and join the heavenly choir? Just as we go into the grave we will come up as far as the character is concerned. For this mortal shall put on immortality and this corruptible shall put on incorruption (see 1 Cor. 15:54). It is the body that will be changed then, but now is the time for washing and ironing. It is the time to wash our robes and make them white in the blood of the Lamb. —Ms 84, 1886.

Ripening for the Harvest

The camp meeting at Worcester, Massachusetts, August 22-28 . . . was an occasion of special interest to me. I there met a large number of believers, some of whom have been connected with the work from the very rise of the third angel's message. Since our last camp meeting, Brother Hastings, one of the faithful standard bearers, had fallen at his post. I felt sad as I saw others weighed down by the infirmities of age, yet I was glad to see them eagerly listening to the words of life. The love of God and His truth seemed to glow in their hearts and to light up their countenances. Their eyes were often filled with tears, not of sorrow but of joy, as they heard the message from God by the mouth of His servants. These aged pilgrims were present at nearly all the meetings, as if they feared that, like Thomas, they might be absent when Jesus should come in, and say, "Peace be unto you."

Like ripening grain these precious tried and faithful ones are fitting for the harvest. Their work is nearly done. They may be permitted to remain till Christ shall be revealed in the clouds of heaven with power and great glory. They may drop out of the ranks at any time, and sleep in Jesus. But while darkness covers the earth and gross darkness the people, these children of the light can lift up their heads and rejoice, knowing that their redemption draweth nigh. —LS 271, 272

THE HOUR OF BEREAVEMENT

No Sin in Weeping

DEAR Sister:
  We sympathize with you in your bereavement and widowhood. I have passed over the ground that you are now traveling, and know what it means. How much sorrow there is in our world! How much grief! How much weeping! It is not right to say to the bereaved ones, "Do not weep; it is not right to weep." Such words have little consolation in them. There is no sin in weeping. Although the one who passes away has been for years a sufferer because of weakness and pain, yet that does not wipe away the tears from our eyes.

Our loved ones die. Their accounts with God are sealed up. But while we consider it a serious, solemn thing to die, we must consider it a much more solemn thing to live. Every day of life is freighted with responsibilities which we must bear. Our individual interests, our words, our actions, are making impressions upon those with whom we are connected. We are to find our consolation in Jesus Christ. Precious Saviour! He was ever touched with human woe. . . . Cling to the Source of your strength. —2SM 264.

The Lord to Be Your Comfort

Dear Sister:
  A letter has just been placed in my hands from Sister G, giving an account of your bereavement. I deeply sympathize with you, my sister. If I were where I could visit you, I would do so. . . .

I will say to you, my sister, the Lord would not have you grieve in sadness. Your husband has been spared to you many years longer than I supposed he would be. God has mercifully spared him, and mercifully, after much suffering, has let him rest in Jesus. . . . Your husband and my husband are at rest. They have no more pain, no more suffering. They are at rest.

I am sorry, my sister, that you are in affliction and sorrow. But Jesus, the precious Saviour, lives. He lives for you. He wants you to be comforted in His love. Do not worry; trust in the Lord. . . . Do not complain. Do not mourn and weep. Do not look on the dark side. Let the peace of God reign in your soul. Then you will have strength to bear all your sufferings, and you will rejoice that you have grace to endure. Praise the Lord; talk of His goodness; tell of His power. Sweeten the atmosphere which surrounds your soul.

Do not dishonor God by words of repining, but praise Him with heart and soul and voice. Look on the bright side of everything. Do not bring a cloud or shadow into your home. Praise Him who is the light of your countenance and your God. Do this, and see how smoothly everything will go. —2SM 266, 267.

Ellen White in Her Hour of Bereavement

In my recent bereavement, I have had a near view of eternity. I have, as it were, been brought before the great white throne, and have seen my life as it will there appear. I can find nothing of which to boast, no merit that I can plead. "Unworthy, unworthy of the least of Thy favors, O my God," is my cry. My only hope is in a crucified and risen Saviour. I claim the merits of the blood of Christ. Jesus will save to the uttermost all who put their trust in Him.

It is sometimes hard for me to preserve a cheerful countenance when my heart is rent with anguish. But I would not permit my sorrow to cast a gloom upon all around me. Seasons of affliction and bereavement are often rendered more sorrowful and distressing than they should be, because it is customary to give ourselves up to mourning without restraint. By the help of Jesus, I determined to shun this evil; but my resolution has been severely tested.

My husband's death was a heavy blow to me, more keenly felt because so sudden. As I saw the seal of death upon his countenance, my feelings were almost insupportable. I longed to cry out in my anguish. But I knew that this could not save the life of my loved one, and I felt that it would be unchristian to give myself up to sorrow. I sought help and comfort from above, and the promises of God were verified to me. The Lord's hand sustained me. It is a sin to indulge, without restraint, in mourning and lamentation. By the grace of Christ, we may be composed and even cheerful under sore trial.

Let us learn a lesson of courage and fortitude from the last interview of Christ with His apostles. They were about to be separated. Our Saviour was entering the blood-stained path which would lead Him to Calvary. Never was scene more trying than that through which He was soon to pass. The apostles had heard the words of Christ foretelling His sufferings and death, and their hearts were heavy with sorrow, their minds distracted with doubt and fear. Yet there were no loud outcries; there was no abandonment of grief. Those last solemn, momentous hours were spent by our Saviour in speaking words of comfort and assurance to His disciples, and then all united in a hymn of praise. —2SM 267, 268.

Ellen Dreams of James Shortly After His Death

A few days since, I was pleading with the Lord for light in regard to my duty. In the night I dreamed I was in the carriage, driving, sitting at the right hand. Father was in the carriage, seated at my left hand. He was very pale, but calm and composed. "Why Father," I exclaimed, "I am so happy to have you by my side once more! I have felt that half of me was gone. Father, I saw you die; I saw you buried. Has the Lord pitied me and let you come back to me again, and we work together as we used to?"

He looked very sad. He said, "The Lord knows what is best for you and for me. My work was very dear to me. We have made a mistake. We have responded to urgent invitations of our brethren to attend important meetings. We had not the heart to refuse. These meetings have worn us both more than we were aware. Our good brethren were gratified, but they did not realize that in these meetings we took upon us greater burdens than at our age we could safely carry. They will never know the result of this long-continued strain upon us. God would have had them bear the burdens we have carried for years. Our nervous energies have been continuously taxed, and then our brethren misjudging our motives and not realizing our burdens have weakened the action of the heart. I have made mistakes, the greatest of which was in allowing my sympathies for the people of God to lead me to take work upon me which others should have borne.

"Now, Ellen, calls will be made as they have been, desiring you to attend important meetings, as has been the case in the past. But lay this matter before God and make no response to the most earnest invitations. Your life hangs as it were upon a thread. You must have quiet rest, freedom from all excitement and from all disagreeable cares. We might have done a great deal for years with our pens, on subjects the people need that we have had light upon and can present before them, which others do not have. Thus you can work when your strength returns, as it will, and you can do far more with your pen than with your voice."

He looked at me appealingly and said, "You will not neglect these cautions, will you, Ellen? Our people will never know under what infirmities we have labored to serve them because our lives were interwoven with the progress of the work, but God knows it all. I regret that I have felt so deeply and labored unreasonably in emergencies, regardless of the laws of life and health. The Lord did not require us to carry so heavy burdens and many of our brethren so few. We ought to have gone to the Pacific Coast before, and devoted our time and energies to writing. Will you do this now? Will you, as your strength returns, take your pen and write out these things we have so long anticipated, and make haste slowly? There is important matter which the people need. Make this your first business. You will have to speak some to the people, but shun the responsibilities which have borne us down."

"Well," said I, "James, you are always to stay with me now and we will work together." Said he, "I stayed in Battle Creek too long. I ought to have gone to California more than one year ago. But I wanted to help the work and institutions at Battle Creek. I have made a mistake. Your heart is tender. You will be inclined to make the same mistakes I have made. Your life can be of use to the cause of God. Oh, those precious subjects the Lord would have had me bring before the people, precious jewels of light!"

I awoke. But this dream seemed so real. Now you can see and understand why I feel no duty to go to Battle Creek for the purpose of shouldering the responsibilities in General Conference. I have no duty to stand in General Conference. The Lord forbids me. That is enough. —Letter 17, 1881.

Vows to Carry On After Husband's Death

During this severe attack of sickness [experienced in Oakland, California, in 1888] I had vividly brought to my remembrance the experience I passed through when my husband was dying. I prayed with him in my great feebleness on that occasion. I sat by his side with his hand in mine until he fell asleep in Jesus. The solemn vows I there made to stand at my post of duty were deeply impressed upon my mind—vows to disappoint the enemy, to bear a constant, earnest appeal to my brethren of the cruelty of their jealousies and evil surmisings which were leavening the churches. I would appeal to them to love one another, to keep their hearts tender by the remembrance of the love of Jesus exercised toward them, in what He did for them. And He said, "Love one another, as I have loved you" (John 15:12). I never can express with pen or voice the work that I discerned was laid out before me on that occasion when I was beside my dying husband. I have not lost the deep views of my work, as I sat by the bed of my husband with his dying hand in mine. —Ms 21, 1888.

Ellen White Reflects on James White's Death

After my husband died, one of our brethren, who thought a great deal of him, said, "Do not let them bury him, but pray to the Lord that He may bring him to life again." I said, "No, no, although I realize my great loss, I will not do this." I felt that he had done his work. No one but myself knew how great a load he had carried in the efforts we had put forth to advance the truth. He had done the work of three men.

Night after night, at the beginning of our work, when advancement seemed to be hindered on every hand, he would say, "Ellen, we must pray. We must not let go until we realize the power of God." He would lie awake for hours, and say, "Oh, Ellen, I am so afflicted. Will you pray for me, that I may not fail or be discouraged." Together we offered up our prayers, with strong crying and tears, until from his lips came the words, "Thank the Lord; He has spoken peace to me. I have light in the Lord. I will not fail. I will press the battle to the gates." Would I have him suffer all this over again? No, no. I would in no case call him from his restful sleep to a life of toil and pain. He will rest until the morning of the resurrection.

My husband died in 1881. During the time that has passed since then, I have missed him constantly. For one year after his death, I felt my loss keenly, until the Lord, when I was at the gates of death, healed me instantly. This was at a camp meeting held at Healdsburg, about a year after my husband's death. Since that time I have been willing to live, or willing to die, just as the Lord sees I can best glorify Him. —Letter 396, 1906.

LESSONS FROM
BIBLE CHARACTERS

The Faith of Abraham

ABRAHAM was an old man when he received the startling command from God to offer up his son Isaac for a burnt offering. Abraham was considered an old man even in his generation. The ardor of his youth had faded away. It was no longer easy for him to endure hardships and brave dangers. In the vigor of youth man may breast the storm with a proud consciousness of strength and rise above discouragements that would cause his heart to fail later in life, when his steps are faltering toward the grave.

But in His providence God reserved His last, most trying, test for Abraham until the burden of years was heavy upon him and he longed for rest from anxiety and toil. The Lord spoke unto him, saying: "Take now thy son, thine only son Isaac, whom thou lovest," "and offer him . . . for a burnt offering." The heart of the old man stood still with horror. The loss of such a son by disease would have been most heart-rending to the fond father; it would have bowed his whitened head with sorrow; but now he is commanded to shed the precious blood of that son with his own hand. It seemed to him a fearful impossibility.

Yet God had spoken, and His word must be obeyed. Abraham was stricken in years, but this did not excuse him from duty. He grasped the staff of faith and in dumb agony took by the hand his child, beautiful in the rosy health of youth, and went out to obey the word of God. The grand old patriarch was human; his passions and attachments were like ours, and he loved his boy, who was the solace of his old age, and to whom the promise of the Lord had been given.

But Abraham did not stop to question how God's promises could be fulfilled if Isaac were slain. He did not stay to reason with his aching heart, but carried out the divine command to the very letter, till, just as the knife was about to be plunged into the quivering flesh of the child, the word came: "Lay not thine hand upon the lad;" "for now I know that thou fearest God, seeing thou hast not withheld thy son, thine only son from Me."

This great act of faith is penciled on the pages of sacred history to shine forth upon the world as an illustrious example to the end of time. Abraham did not plead that his old age should excuse him from obeying God. He did not say: "My hairs are gray, the vigor of my manhood is gone; who will comfort my waning life when Isaac is no more? How can an aged father spill the blood of an only son?" No; God had spoken, and man must obey without questioning, murmuring, or fainting by the way.

We need the faith of Abraham in our churches today, to lighten the darkness that gathers around them, shutting out the sweet sunlight of God's love and dwarfing spiritual growth. Age will never excuse us from obeying God. Our faith should be prolific of good works, for faith without works is dead. Every duty performed, every sacrifice made in the name of Jesus, brings an exceeding great reward. In the very act of duty, God speaks and gives His blessing. But He requires of us an entire surrender of the faculties. The mind and heart, the whole being, must be given to Him, or we fall short of becoming true Christians. — 4T 144, 145.

David's Prayer

I was shown David entreating the Lord not to forsake him when he should be old, and what it was that called forth his earnest prayer. He saw that most of the aged around him were unhappy and that unhappy traits of character increased especially with age. If persons were naturally close and covetous, they were most disagreeably so in their old age. If they were jealous, fretful, and impatient, they were especially so when aged.

David was distressed as he saw that kings and nobles who seemed to have the fear of God before them while in the strength of manhood, became jealous of their best friends and relatives when aged. They were in continual fear that it was selfish motives which led their friends to manifest an interest for them. They would listen to the hints and the deceptive advice of strangers in regard to those in whom they should confide. Their unrestrained jealousy sometimes burned into a flame because all did not agree with their failing judgment. Their covetousness was dreadful. They often thought that their own children and relatives were wishing them to die in order to take their place and possess their wealth, and receive the homage which had been bestowed upon them. And some were so controlled by their jealous, covetous feelings as to destroy their own children.

David marked that although the lives of some while in the strength of manhood had been righteous, as old age came upon them they seemed to lose their self-control. Satan stepped in and guided their minds, making them restless and dissatisfied. He saw that many of the aged seemed forsaken of God and exposed themselves to the ridicule and reproaches of his enemies. David was deeply moved; he was distressed as he looked forward to the time when he should be aged. He feared that God would leave him and that he would be as unhappy as other aged persons whose course he had noticed, and would be left to the reproach of the enemies of the Lord.

With this burden upon him he earnestly prays: "Cast me not off in the time of old age; forsake me not when my strength faileth." "O God, Thou hast taught me from my youth: and hitherto have I declared Thy wondrous works. Now also when I am old and gray-headed, O God, forsake me not; until I have showed Thy strength unto this generation, and Thy power to everyone that is to come" [Ps. 71:9, 17, 18]. David felt the necessity of guarding against the evils which attend old age. —1T 422, 423

David Planned Ahead

David, in arranging his business, sets a good example to all who are advanced in years, to settle their matters while they are capable of doing so, that when they shall be drawing near to death, and their mental faculties are dimmed, they shall have nothing of a worldly nature to divert their minds from God. — 2BC 1025.

How Peter Faced Death

Since his reinstatement after his denial of Christ, Peter had unflinchingly braved danger, and had shown a noble courage and boldness in preaching a crucified, risen, and ascended Saviour. As he lay in his cell, he called to mind the words that Christ had spoken to him: "Verily, verily, I say unto thee, When thou wast young, thou girdedst thyself, and walkedst whither thou wouldest: but when thou shalt be old, thou shalt stretch forth thy hands, and another shall gird thee, and carry thee whither thou wouldest not." Thus Jesus had made known to the disciple the very manner of his death, and even foretold the stretching of his hands upon the cross.

Peter, as a Jew and a foreigner, was condemned to be scourged and crucified. In prospect of this fearful death, the apostle remembered his great sin in denying Jesus in the hour of His trial. Once so unready to acknowledge the cross, he now counted it a joy to yield up his life for the gospel, feeling only that for him who had denied his Lord, to die in the same manner as his Master died was too great an honor. Peter had sincerely repented of that sin, and had been forgiven by Christ, as is shown by the high commission given him to feed the sheep and lambs of the flock. But he could never forgive himself. Not even the thought of the agonies of the last terrible scene could lessen the bitterness of his sorrow and repentance. As a last favor, he entreated his executioners that he might be nailed to the cross with his head downward. The request was granted, and in this manner died the great apostle Peter. —RH Sept. 26, 1912. (See also AA 537, 538)

The Aged Apostle on Patmos

More than half a century had passed since the organization of the Christian church. During that time the gospel message had been constantly opposed. Its enemies had never relaxed their efforts, and had at last succeeded in enlisting the power of the Roman emperor against the Christians.

In the terrible persecution that followed, the apostle John did much to confirm and strengthen the faith of the believers. He bore a testimony which his adversaries could not controvert, and which helped his brethren to meet with courage and loyalty the trials that came upon them. When the faith of the Christians would seem to waver under the fierce opposition they were forced to meet, the old, tried servant of Jesus would repeat with power and eloquence the story of the crucified and risen Saviour. He steadfastly maintained his faith, and from his lips came ever the same glad message: "That which was from the beginning, which we have heard, which we have seen with our eyes, which we have looked upon, and our hands have handled, of the Word of life; . . . that which we have seen and heard declare we unto you."

John lived to be very old. He witnessed the destruction of Jerusalem and the ruin of the stately temple. The last survivor of the disciples who had been intimately connected with the Saviour, his message had great influence in setting forth the fact that Jesus was the Messiah, the Redeemer of the world. No one could doubt his sincerity, and through his teachings many were continually turning from unbelief.

The rulers of the Jews were filled with bitter hatred against John for his unwavering fidelity to the cause of Christ. They declared that their efforts against the Christians would avail nothing so long as John's testimony kept ringing in the ears of the people. In order that the miracles and teachings of Jesus might be forgotten, the voice of the bold witness must be silenced.

John was accordingly summoned to Rome to be tried for his faith. Here before the authorities the apostle's doctrines were misstated. False witnesses accused him of teaching seditious heresies. By these accusations his enemies hoped to bring about the disciple's death.

John answered for himself in a clear and convincing manner, and with such simplicity and candor that his words had a powerful effect. His hearers were astonished at his wisdom and eloquence. But the more convincing his testimony, the deeper was the hatred of his opposers. The emperor Domitian was filled with rage. He could not dispute the reasoning of Christ's faithful advocate, nor match the power that attended his utterance of truth; yet he determined that he would silence his voice.

John was cast into a caldron of boiling oil: but the Lord preserved the life of His faithful servant, even as He preserved the three Hebrews in the fiery furnace. As the words were spoken, "Thus perish all who believe in that deceiver, Jesus Christ of Nazareth," John declared, "My Master patiently submitted to all that Satan and his angels could devise to humiliate and torture Him. He gave His life to save the world. I am honored in being permitted to suffer for His sake. I am a weak, sinful man. Christ was holy, harmless, undefiled. He did not sin, neither was guile found in His mouth." These words had their influence, and John was removed from the caldron by the very men who had cast him in.

Again the hand of persecution fell heavily upon the apostle. By the emperor's decree, John was banished to the isle of Patmos, condemned, "for the word of God, and for the testimony of Jesus Christ." Here, his enemies thought, his influence would no longer be felt, and he must finally die of hardship and distress.

To outward appearance, the enemies of truth were triumphing, but God's hand was moving unseen in the darkness. God permitted His faithful servant to be placed where Christ could give him a more wonderful revelation of Himself, and of divine truth for the enlightenment of the churches. In exiling John the enemies of truth had hoped to silence forever the voice of the faithful disciple; but on Patmos he received a message, the influence of which his enemies could not destroy, and which was to continue to strengthen the church to the end of time. Though not released from the responsibility of their wrong act, those who exiled John became instruments in the hands of God to carry out His purpose; and the very effort to extinguish the light placed the truth in bold relief.

Patmos, a barren, rocky island in the Aegean Sea, had been chosen by the Roman government as a place of banishment for criminals; but to the servant of God this gloomy abode became the gate of heaven. Here, shut away from the busy scenes of life, and from the active labors of former years, he had the companion-ship of God and Christ and the heavenly angels, and from them he received instruction for the church for all future time. The events that would take place in the closing scenes of this earth's history were outlined before him; and there he wrote out the visions he received from God. When his voice could no longer testify to the One whom he loved and served, the messages given him on that barren coast were to go forth as a lamp that burneth, declaring the sure purpose of the Lord concerning every nation on the earth.

Among the cliffs and rocks of Patmos, John held communion with his Maker. He reviewed his past life, and at thought of the blessings he had received, peace filled his heart. He had lived the life of a Christian, and he could say in faith, "We know that we have passed from death unto life." Not so the emperor who had banished him. He could look back only on fields of warfare and carnage, on desolated homes, on weeping widows and orphans, the fruit of his ambitious desire for pre-eminence.

In his isolated home John was able to study more closely than ever before the manifestations of divine power as recorded in the book of nature and in the pages of inspiration. To him it was a delight to meditate on the work of creation, and to adore the divine Architect.

In former years his eyes had been greeted by the sight of forest-covered hills, green valleys, and fruitful plains; and in the beauties of nature it had ever been his delight to trace the wisdom and skill of the Creator. He was now surrounded by scenes that to many would appear gloomy and uninteresting; but to John it was otherwise. While his surroundings might be desolate and barren, the blue heavens that bent above him were as bright and beautiful as the skies above his loved Jerusalem. In the wild, rugged rocks, in the mysteries of the deep, in the glories of the firmament, he read important lessons. All bore the message of God's power and glory.

All around him the apostle beheld witnesses to the flood that had deluged the earth because the inhabitants ventured to transgress the law of God. The rocks thrown up from the great deep and from the earth, by the breaking forth of the waters, brought vividly to his mind the terrors of that awful outpouring of God's wrath. In the voice of many waters—deep calling unto deep—the prophet heard the voice of the Creator. The sea, lashed to fury by the merciless winds, represented to him the wrath of an offended God. The mighty waves, in their terrible commotion, restrained within limits appointed by an invisible hand, spoke of the control of an infinite Power. And in contrast he realized the weakness and folly of mortals, who, though but worms of the dust, glory in their supposed wisdom and strength, and set their hearts against the Ruler of the universe, as if God were altogether such a one as themselves. By the rocks he was reminded of Christ, the Rock of his strength, in whose shelter he could hide without fear. From the exiled apostle on rocky Patmos there went up the most ardent longing of soul after God, the most fervent prayers. —RH Sept. 5, 1912. (See also AA 568-572)

The Best Time of John's Life

The history of John affords a striking illustration of the way in which God can use aged workers. When John was exiled to the isle of Patmos, there were many who thought him to be past service, an old and broken reed, ready to fall at any time. But the Lord saw fit to use him still. Though banished from the scenes of his former labor, he did not cease to bear witness to the truth. Even in Patmos he made friends and converts. His was a message of joy, proclaiming a risen Saviour who on high was interceding for His people until He should return to take them to Himself. And it was after John had grown old in the service of his Lord that he received more communications from heaven than he had received during all the former years of his life. —AA 572, 573.

In his old age John revealed the life of Christ in his life. He lived to be nearly one hundred years old, and over and over again he repeated the story of the crucified and risen Saviour. Persecution came upon the believers, and those young in experience were often in danger of losing their hold on Christ. But the old, tried servant of Jesus steadfastly maintained his faith. —7BC 947.

Comfort From Experiences of Bible Characters

In the experience of the apostle John during his

persecution, there is a lesson of wonderful strength and comfort for the people of God. God does not prevent the plottings of wicked men, but He causes their devices to work for good to those who in trial and conflict maintain their faith and loyalty. Often the gospel worker carries on his work amid storms of persecution, bitter opposition, and unjust reproach. At such times let him remember that the experience to be gained in the furnace of trial and affliction is worth more than all the pain it costs. Thus God brings His children near to Him, that He may show them their weakness and His strength. He teaches them to lean on Him. Thus He prepares them to meet emergencies, to fill positions of trust, and to accomplish the great purpose for which their powers were given them.

In all ages, God's appointed witnesses have exposed themselves to reproach and persecution for the truth's sake. Joseph was maligned and persecuted because he preserved his virtue and integrity. David, the chosen messenger of God, was hunted like a beast of prey by his enemies. Daniel was cast into a den of lions because he was true to his allegiance to heaven. Job was deprived of his worldly possessions, and so afflicted in body that he was abhorred by his relatives and friends; yet he maintained his integrity. Jeremiah could not be deterred from speaking the words that God had given him to speak; and his testimony so enraged the king and princes that he was cast into a loathsome pit. Stephen was stoned because he preached Christ and Him crucified. Paul was imprisoned, beaten with rods, stoned, and finally put to death because he was a faithful messenger for God to the Gentiles. And John was banished to the isle of Patmos "for the word of God, and for the testimony of Jesus Christ."

These examples of human steadfastness bear witness to the faithfulness of God's promises—of His abiding presence and sustaining grace. They testify to the power of faith to withstand the powers of the world. It is the work of faith to rest in God in the darkest hour, to feel, however sorely tried and tempest tossed, that our Father is at the helm. The eye of faith alone can look beyond the things of time to estimate aright the worth of eternal riches. —RH Sept. 12, 1912. (See also AA 574-576)

Solomon's Life of Backsliding

The life of Solomon is full of warning, not only to youth, but to those of mature years and to the aged, those who are descending the hill of life and facing the western sun. . . .

When Solomon should have been in character as a sturdy oak, he fell from his steadfastness under the power of temptation. When his strength should have been the firmest, he was found the weakest of men.

From such examples as this we should learn that watchfulness and prayer are the only safety for either young or old. Satan will so shape circumstances that unless we are kept by divine power they will almost imperceptibly weaken the fortifications of the soul. We need to inquire at every step, "Is this the way of the Lord?"

As long as life shall last, there is need of guarding the affections and the passions with a firm purpose.

There is inward corruption, there are outward temptations, and wherever the work of God shall be advanced, Satan plans so to arrange circumstances that temptation shall come with overpowering force upon the soul. Not one moment can we be secure, only as we are relying upon God, the life hid with Christ in God.

Notwithstanding the warnings in the Word of God and in the testimonies of His Spirit, many have closed their eyes to danger and have gone on in their own way, infatuated, deluded by Satan until they fall under his temptations. Then they abandon themselves to despair. This was the history of Solomon. But even for him there was help. He truly repented of his course of sin, and found help.

Let none venture into sin as he did, in the hope that they too may recover themselves. Sin can be indulged only at the peril of infinite loss. But none who have fallen need give themselves up to despair. Aged men, once honored of God, may have defiled their souls, sacrificing virtue on the altar of lust; but there is still hope for them if they repent, forsake sin, and turn to God.

The misapplication of noble talents in Solomon's case should be a warning to all. . . . His history stands as a beacon of warning that young and old may learn the sure result of departure from the ways of the Lord.

Solomon acted in direct opposition to God's will. God had made him the depositary of sacred truths, but he proved unfaithful to his holy trust. Evil communications corrupted good manners. He entered into political alliance with pagan kingdoms, especially with Egypt and Phoenicia. One wrong step led to another. Through his associations with these nations, their heathen practices became less abhorrent to him, and at last their sensual customs and their darkest worships were imported into Palestine. Solomon's fine sensibilities were blunted, his conscience scared. He became weak and vacillating. The justice of his early reign gave place to tyranny. Once the guardian of his people, he became a despot. To support his extravagance and profligacy he imposed a grinding taxation upon the poor.

He who had said to his people at the dedication of the temple, "Let your heart therefore be perfect with the Lord our God," became himself the offender. In heart and life he denied his own words. He mistook license for liberty. He tried, but at what cost, to unite light with darkness, Christ with Belial, purity with impurity, good with evil. Shall we give heed to the warning, and shun the first approach to those sins which overcame him who was called the wisest of men?—Letter 8b, 1891.

Solomon's Weakness
a Beacon of Warning

Of Solomon the inspired record says, "His wives turned away his heart after other gods: and his heart was not perfect with the Lord his God."

This is no theme to be treated with a smile. The heart that loves Jesus will not desire the unlawful affections of another. Every want is supplied in Christ. This superficial affection is of the same character as that exalted enjoyment which Satan promised Eve. It is coveting that which God has forbidden. When it is too late hundreds can warn others not to venture upon the precipice. Intellect, position, wealth can never, never take the place of moral qualities. Clean hands, a pure heart, and noble, earnest devotion to God and the truth the Lord esteems above the golden wedge of Ophir.

An evil influence has a perpetuating power. I wish I could set this matter before God's commandment-keeping people just as it has been shown me. Let the sad memory of Solomon's apostasy warn every soul to shun the same precipice. His weakness and sin are handed down from generation to generation. The greatest king that ever wielded a scepter, of whom it had been said that he was the beloved of God, through misplaced affection became contaminated and was miserably forsaken of his God. The mightiest ruler of the earth had failed to rule his own passions. Solomon may have been saved "as by fire," yet his repentance could not efface those high places, nor demolish those stones, which remained as evidences of his crimes. He dishonored God, choosing rather to be controlled by lust than to be a partaker of the divine nature.

What a legacy Solomon's life has committed to those who would use his example to cover their own base actions. We must either transmit a heritage of good or evil. Shall our lives and our example be a blessing or a curse? Shall people look at our graves and say, "He ruined me," or "He saved me"? . . .

The lesson to be learned from the life of Solomon has a special moral bearing upon the life of the aged, of those who are no longer climbing the mountain but are descending and facing the western sun. We expect to see defects in the characters of youth who are not controlled by love and faith in Jesus Christ. We see youth wavering between right and wrong, vacillating between fixed principle and the almost overpowering current of evil that is bearing them off their feet to ruin. But of those of mature age we expect better things. We look for the character to be established, for principles to be rooted, and for them to be beyond the danger of pollution.

But the case of Solomon is before us as a beacon of warning. When thou, aged pilgrim who hast fought the battles of life, thinkest that thou standest, take heed lest thou fall. How, in Solomon's case, was weak, vacillating character, naturally bold, firm, and determined, shaken like a reed in the wind under the tempter's power! How was an old gnarled cedar of Lebanon, a sturdy oak of Bashan, bent before the blast of temptation! What a lesson for all who desire to save their souls to watch unto prayer continually! What a warning to keep the grace of Christ ever in their heart, to battle with inward corruptions and outward temptations!— 2BC 1031, 1032.

Worldly Renown Versus Godly Integrity

It has been said of men of gray hairs that there is no danger of their shrinking from their post of duty; but in the case of Solomon, when he became old, we learn that he lost his connection with God. And why?— Because he sought after the renown, honor, and riches of this world; because he took wives from among the idolatrous nations, and became allied with those nations. It is true that by this alliance he brought gold from Ophir and silver from Tarshish; but it was at the expense of virtue, of principle, of integrity of character.

All through the history of the Jewish nation we see that the people of God, whether old or young, had to keep themselves distinct and separate from the idolatrous nations around them. God has a people today; and it is just as necessary now as anciently that His people should keep themselves distinct and separate, pure and unspotted from the world, its spirit, and its influences, because the world sets up a standard opposed to the standard of truth and righteousness. —RH Jan. 4, 1887.

Influence for Good or for Ill

Solomon's repentance was sincere; but the harm that his example of evil-doing had wrought, could not be undone. During his apostasy, there were in the kingdom men who remained true to their trust, maintaining their purity and loyalty. But many were led astray; and the forces of evil set in operation by the introduction of idolatry and worldly practices, could not easily be stayed by the penitent king. His influence for good was greatly weakened. Many hesitated to place full confidence in his leadership. Though the king confessed his sin, and wrote out, for the benefit of after generations, a record of his folly and repentance, he could never hope entirely to destroy the baleful influence of his wrong deeds. Emboldened by his apostasy, many continued to do evil, and evil only. And in the downward course of many of the rulers who followed him, may be traced the sad influence of the prostitution of his God-given powers. . . .

Among the many lessons taught by Solomon's life, none is more strongly emphasized than the power of influence for good or for ill. However contracted may be our sphere, we still exert an influence for weal or woe. Beyond our knowledge or control, it tells upon others in blessing or cursing. It may be heavy with the gloom of discontent and selfishness, or poisonous with the deadly taint of some cherished sin; or it may be charged with the life-giving power of faith, courage, and hope, and sweet with the fragrance of love. But potent for good or for ill it will surely be. —PK 84, 85.

APPENDIX A

HELPFUL BIBLE TEXTS FOR SENIORS

AND thou shalt go to thy fathers in peace; thou shalt be buried in a good old age. —Gen. 15:15.

Thou shalt rise up before the hoary head, and honor the face of the old man, and fear thy God: I am the Lord. —Lev. 19:32.

And king Rehoboam consulted with the old men, that stood before Solomon his father while he yet lived, and said, How do ye advise that I may answer this people?

And they spake unto him, saying, If thou wilt be a servant unto this people this day, and wilt serve them, and answer them, and speak good words to them, then they will be thy servants for ever.

But he forsook the counsel of the old men, which they had given him, and consulted with the young men that were grown up with him, and which stood before him: . . .

And the king answered the people roughly, and forsook the old men's counsel that they gave him;

And spake to them after the counsel of the young men, saying, My father made your yoke heavy, and I will add to your yoke: my father also chastised you with whips, but I will chastise you with scorpions. . . .

So Israel rebelled against the house of David unto this day. —1 Kings 12:6-8, 13, 14, 19.

With the ancient is wisdom; and in length of days understanding. —Job 12:12.

Yea, though I walk through the valley of the shadow of death, I will fear no evil: for Thou art with me; Thy rod and Thy staff they comfort me. — Ps. 23:4.

Cast me not off in the time of old age; forsake me not when my strength faileth. —Ps. 71:9.

Forsake me not, O God, when I am old and gray; that I may tell the rising generation of Thy strength and Thy might. — Ps. 71:18, Moffatt.

The days of our years are threescore years and ten; and if by reason of strength they be fourscore years, yet is their strength labor and sorrow. . . .

So teach us to number our days, that we may apply our hearts unto wisdom. —Ps. 90:10, 12.

They shall still bring forth fruit in old age; they shall be fat and flourishing; to shew that the Lord is upright: He is my rock, and there is no unrighteousness in Him. —Ps. 92:14, 15.

Praise the Lord from the earth, . . .

Both young men, and maidens; old men, and children:

Let them praise the name of the Lord: for His name alone is excellent; His glory is above the earth and heaven. —Ps. 148:7, 12, 13.

Children's children are the crown of old men; and the glory of children are their fathers. —Prov. 17:6.

The glory of young men is their strength: and the beauty of old men is the gray head. —Prov. 20:29.

It is a wonderful thing to be alive! —Eccl. 11:7, The Living Bible.

If a man live many years, let him have joy throughout them all; let him remember that the dark days will be many—Eccl. 11:8, Moffatt.

Don't let the excitement of being young cause you to forget about your Creator. Honor Him in your youth before the evil years come—when you'll no longer enjoy living.

It will be too late then to try to remember Him, when the sun and light and moon and stars are dim to your old eyes, and there is no silver lining left among your clouds.

For there will come a time when your limbs will tremble with age, and your strong legs will become weak, and your teeth will be too few to do their work, and there will be blindness, too.

Then let your lips be tightly closed while eating, when your teeth are gone! And you will waken at dawn with the first note of the birds; but you yourself will be deaf and tuneless, with quavering voice.

You will be afraid of heights and of falling—a white-haired, withered old man, dragging himself along: without sexual desire, standing at death's door, and nearing his everlasting home as the mourners go along the streets.

Yes, remember your Creator now while you are young, before the silver cord of life snaps, and the golden bowl is broken, and the pitcher is broken at the fountain, and the wheel is broken at the cistern;

And the dust returns to the earth as it was, and the spirit returns to God Who gave it. . . .

Here is my final conclusion: fear God and obey His commandments, for this is the entire duty of man.

For God will judge us for everything we do, including every hidden thing, good or bad. —Eccl. 12:1-7, 13, 14, The Living Bible.

In returning and rest shall ye be saved; in quietness and in confidence shall be your strength. – Isa. 30:15.

Even the youths shall faint and be weary, and the young men shall utterly fall: but they that wait upon the Lord shall renew their strength; they shall mount up with wings as eagles; they shall run, and not be weary; and they shall walk, and not faint. —Isa. 40:30, 31.

Even to your old age I will be the same, when you are gray-haired, still I will sustain you; I have borne the burden, I will carry it, yes, I will carry you and save you. —Isa. 46:4, Moffatt.

And it shall come to pass afterward, that I will pour out My spirit upon all flesh; and your sons and your daughters shall prophesy, your old men shall dream dreams, your young men shall see visions. —Joel 2:28.

When I sit in darkness, the Lord shall be a light unto me. —Micah 7:8.

Thus saith the Lord of hosts; There shall yet old men and old women dwell in the streets of Jerusalem, and every man with his staff in his hand for very age.

And the streets of the city shall be full of boys and girls playing in the streets thereof. —Zech. 8:4, 5.

At evening time it shall be light. —Zech. 14:7.

There was in the days of Herod, the king of Judaea, a certain priest named Zacharias, of the course of Abia; and his wife was of the daughters of Aaron, and her name was Elisabeth.

And they were both righteous before God, walking

in all the commandments and ordinances of the Lord blameless.

And they had no child, because that Elisabeth was barren, and they both were now well stricken in years. . . .

And there appeared unto him an angel of the Lord standing on the right side of the altar of incense.

And when Zacharias saw him, he was troubled, and fear fell upon him.

But the angel said unto him, Fear not, Zacharias: for thy prayer is heard; and thy wife Elisabeth shall bear thee a son, and thou shalt call his name John. . . .

And his father Zacharias was filled with the Holy Ghost, and prophesied, saying,

Blessed be the Lord God of Israel; for He hath visited and redeemed His people. —Luke 1:5-7, 11-13, 67, 68.

And, behold, there was a man in Jerusalem, whose name was Simeon; and the same man was just and devout, waiting for the consolation of Israel: and the Holy Ghost was upon him.

And it was revealed unto him by the Holy Ghost, that he should not see death, before he had seen the Lord's Christ.

And he came by the Spirit into the temple: and when the parents brought in the child Jesus, to do for Him after the custom of the law,

Then took he Him up in his arms, and blessed God, and said,

Lord, now lettest Thou Thy servant depart in peace, according to Thy word:

For mine eyes have seen Thy salvation,

Which Thou hast prepared before the face of all people;

A light to lighten the Gentiles, and the glory of Thy people Israel. —Luke 2:25-32.

And there was one Anna, a prophetess, the daughter of Phanuel, of the tribe of Aser: she was of a great age, and had lived with an husband seven years from her virginity;

And she was a widow of about fourscore and four years, which departed not from the temple, but served God with fastings and prayers night and day.

And she coming in that instant gave thanks likewise unto the Lord, and spake of Him to all them that looked for redemption in Jerusalem. —Luke 2:36-38.

That the aged men be sober, grave, temperate, sound in faith, in charity, in patience.

The aged women likewise, that they be in behavior as becometh holiness, not false accusers, not given to much wine, teachers of good things;

That they may teach the young women to be sober, to love their husbands, to love their children,

To be discreet, chaste, keepers at home, good, obedient to their own husbands, that the word of God be not blasphemed. —Titus 2:2-5.

Come, then, stiffen your drooping arms and shaking knees, and keep your steps from wavering. Then the disabled limb will not be put out of joint, but regain its former powers. —Heb. 12:12, 13, New English Bible.

APPENDIX B

A BRIEF SUMMARY OF
ELLEN WHITE'S ACTIVITIES
AFTER AGE 65

1893

LIVED at George's Terrace, Melbourne, in Jan. Labored in Melbourne area, at the school and publishing house and area churches. Attended fifth annual session of Australian Conf. in North Fitzroy, Melbourne, Jan. 6-15. Left for Sydney Jan. 26, en route to New Zealand, accompanied by Emily Campbell and Elder and Mrs. Starr. Spent a week with church at Parramatta, near Sydney, and spoke 5 times. Sailed for New Zealand Feb. 4; landed in Auckland Feb. 8 and spent 12 days laboring for church there; sailed for Kaeo Feb. 20, arrived Feb. 22 and labored there Feb. 22-March 15, staying in home of Joseph Hare. Returned to Auckland March 17 and proceeded to Napier for workers' meeting and camp meeting, March 22-April 6. Met appointment at Hastings April 2, and labored for Sabbathkeepers in Palmerston North following Napier meetings.

Made her home in Wellington, in home of Sr. Tuxford, from early April to mid-August, having dental work cared for, writing, and laboring in nearby places—Mentone, Petone, and Paremata (with the

---

* Drawn from the White Estate Biographical file on the life of Ellen G. White. The abbreviated form in which these notations appear on the index cards has been retained here. For greater detail, see the *Comprehensive Index to the Writings of Ellen G. White*, vol. 3, pp. 2964-2969.

Brown family). Made Hastings her headquarters mid-Aug. through Sept., alternating between Hastings and Napier churches; also met appointments in Ormondville and Norsewood. Spent a few weeks in Gisborne. Returned to Wellington late Nov., for second New Zealand camp meeting, — "three weeks of solid labor." Sailed for Sydney Dec. 14, spoke to Auckland church Friday eve. and Sabbath, before sailing from there; rough voyage, no writing done. Reached Sydney Dec. 22 and hastened to Melbourne to attend first camp meeting in Australia, beginning Dec. 29.

1894

On campground, Middle Brighton, Melbourne, as year opened. Labored in workers' meeting, camp meeting, and Australian Union Conf. session till late Jan., returning to the school (at George's Terrace) for treatments on alternate days. At George's Terrace through Feb. and until late March, laboring in area churches—Williamstown, North Brighton, Prahan, George's Terrace. Moved from Melbourne to Granville, near Sydney, March 27. Labored for believers in Sydney area—Parramatta, Kellyville, Seven Hills, city of Sydney, Castle Hill, Granville. In late May visited Dora Creek, site being considered for school.

Moved from her first Granville home to another —Norfolk Villa—last week in June, and continued her labors in neighboring churches. Visited Cooranbong late in August; pleased with the land for school. May Walling returned to U.S. to appear in connection with

Walling suit. Labored in second Australian camp meeting, in Ashfield, a suburb of Sydney, in October. Drove to Pennant Hills for speaking appointment Nov. 25, a meeting which was to be the beginning of a series of meetings. Location of school, supposedly settled, was resurrected, and Dec. 13 she was called to visit Fairlight as another possible location; not practicable to locate there. Many guests were entertained in her Granville home—workers coming for counsel or passing through to go to Cooranbong. *Christian Education* was published in 1894.

1895

Norfolk Villa, Granville. Took provisions to James family. Gave a "lift" to strangers needing a ride, and "had a very pleasant acquaintance." Stopped carriage while Emily got out and separated two little girls who were "fighting like a couple of dogs." Trying to sell Battle Creek property. Spoke at Ashfield Sabbath, Jan. 12, took dinner at Bro. Corliss', then drove to Sydney and read the words the Lord had given her for Brn. Hardy and Humphrey, and presented the need of the truth in Sydney, and evil of criticism, etc. "Spoke plainly"; meeting lasted till after 6 p.m. Home about 8, very tired, heart heavy. Jan. 14 left with May Lacey and Maude Camp for Cooranbong, for girls to learn dressmaking from Sister Rousseau. Maintained her home in Granville till late in Dec., 1895. Exhausted from much labor, as year began—labor and almost continuous company.

Visited Cooranbong (now accepted as school site),

Jan. 14-23, for rest, accompanied by May Lacey and Maud Camp. Continued her labors among the churches—Ashfield (where a tent meeting was in progress in Jan.), Sydney, Petersham, Prospect, Parramatta. Left Granville April 11, spent Sabbath in Melbourne, and sailed for Tasmania April 16, accompanied by May Lacey. WCW had preceded them, and met them in Hobart. Entertained in Lacey home, and met appointments in Hobart and Bismark.

WCW and May Lacey were married in the Lacey home May 9, and with EGW left that night for Launceston, where EGW spoke both Sabbath and Sunday. (Ella and Mabel White had arrived in Sydney about May 5.) Returned to Melbourne May 14 or 15, and spent remainder of month in labors in area—at Williamstown, Brighton, North Fitzroy, Hawthorne. Back in her Granville home during June, speaking on Sabbaths and Sundays in the area, driving several miles to meet these appointments. Canterbury was added to the list about this time. Most of these meetings were held in halls or tents, but soon efforts were being put forth to build churches.

With W.C.W. and wife and Ella and Mabel, went to Cooranbong July 1, for rest. Spoke Sabbath July 6 and 13. Bought 40 acres from the school and planned to make her home there. Returned to Granville in mid-July, but was back in Cooranbong during most of August, living in tent, supervising planting of her orchard, and getting her new home started.

Returned to Granville in early Sept. Much exhausted. Sara McEnterfer arrived from U.S. Oct. 15.

Continued her labors in Sydney area in spite of weakness, and labored in third Australian camp meeting, at Armadale, Melbourne, Oct. 18-Nov. 21, and in Tasmanian camp meeting, at Hobart, in Dec. Returned to her Granville home Dec. 20, and arrived at her new home at Avondale, Cooranbong, Dec. 25. Family consisted of Marian Davis, Sara M., Maggie Hare, May Israel, Sarah Belden, Edith Ward, and Bro. Connell—and E.G.W. Temporary structure was being planned for W.C.W. and family.

1896

At her new home in Cooranbong ("Sunnyside") the greater portion of the year, engrossed in writing, speaking, and counseling with the workers re development of the school. Visited Sydney in March and spoke in Ashfield church; also in September. Attended and labored in camp meeting in Adelaide in October, accompanied by W.C.W. and Sara M. Spoke in Newtown and Ashfield en route to Adelaide. Left Adelaide Oct. 19, with Sara M. and Elder Haskell. Stopped off in Ballarat for appointment, and thence to Melbourne, where she spent about two weeks and spoke several times in area churches, including the "new church" at North Fitzroy.

Labored in the second conf. meeting of the New South Wales Conf. (of which W.C.W. was president) in Ashfield, in Nov. Returned to "Sunnyside" in late Nov. quite ill, suffered intensely for two weeks and was unable to attend meetings for a time. Spoke to the people from her phaeton, out-of-doors, on the last evening of the year. *Thoughts From the Mount of Blessing* and *Christ Our Saviour* were published in 1896.

1897

At her "Sunnyside" home. Spoke "in the chamber above the mill" on Sabbath, Jan. 2 (for first time since her illness late in 1896). "We must have a meeting-house," she decided—and she inspired interest and effort until the meetinghouse was a reality. Planning to build a home for W.C.W.'s family. Counseling with Bro. Semmens re a Health Home.

Visited Summer Hill (to counsel with Brethren Semmens and Haskell re Health Home), and met speaking appointments in Newtown and Ashfield—all in Sydney area, in Feb. Carrying heavy burdens in connection with the school, counseling in regard to many problems, speaking frequently, etc. Also oversee-ing building of home for W.C.W.'s family, while he was in U.S. for Gen. Conf.

Visited Summer Hill, Sydney, Ashfield, and New-town again in August, speaking and counseling, and spent a few days in Summer Hill in Sept. Spoke fre-quently to the students, and on Sabbaths "in the crowded upper chamber." Oct. 16 spoke in the new chapel, and Oct. 17 offered dedicatory prayer at the dedication of the new chapel—a triumph of faith.

Labored in camp meeting at Stanmore, near Syd-ney, Oct. 21-31. Returned to "Sunnyside" Nov. 1, feeling very ill. Deeply interested in the work at Stan-more, and labored there again Nov. 19-23, Dec. 3-6 and 17-27. Plans were under way for a church building there. Met W.C.W. at Stanmore Oct. 21, he having just returned from 10 months' absence in U.S. Many sick came for help; Sara M. proved to be a real medical missionary, answering many calls for help; at times the sick were cared for in E.G.W.'s home.

1898

At "Sunnyside," burdened with writing and counseling, and passing through a period of anxiety, heartache, and perplexity re her duty. "Feel that I shall have to go to America and bear my testimony once more. . . ." Labored in Stanmore again Jan. 2-5 and Jan 27-Feb. 2. Also spoke at Ashfield Jan. 31. A tent effort was on in Stanmore at this time, in which she assisted.

In Melbourne area late Feb. to early April; spoke 8 times in the tent in Balaclava, 3 times to No. Fitzroy church also to office workers; met weekend appointments in Geelong and in Ballarat. Labored under difficulties, as she was suffering from malaria, but though she spoke "in a feeble voice" on Sabbath at Ballarat, she was strengthened on Sunday to speak in a large hall for more than an hour and "was not the least weary."

Was in Sydney area over two Sabbaths in April, where the new Stanmore church was dedicated April 23 (24?). Returned home to Sunnyside April 25, after absence from her "pleasant home" for 2 months. Had spoken 22 times, and done much writing. Labored in Week of Prayer meetings in June, both in meetings for the students and for the church. Busy with writing, and many matters. Aged Bro. Tucker, who had lived in her home for 1 1/2 years, died there June 24. Met speaking appointments in Stanmore weekend of July 7-11, and returned to Stanmore for N.S.W. Conf., meeting July 21-27.

Attended Queensland camp meeting Oct. 13-31, and following camp meeting spent a few days with the Rockhampton church, though weak and ill (and the trip was not an easy one). Canceled plans to stop in Toowoomba for a weekend, and returned to Cooranbong and home Nov. 10, weak and exhausted, "but with quiet and rest I shall grow strong again." Filled appointment at Awaba Nov. 20, spoke to students Nov. 25, and to the church Nov. 26. Labored in camp meeting in Hamilton, Newcastle, in closing days of December. *The Desire of Ages* was published in 1898.

1899

Remained in Newcastle for closing of camp meeting, Jan. 2, and a few days of follow-up work. Much exhausted following this camp meeting but labored at home as able, writing and counseling. Labored at Newcastle again Feb. 3-5 and Feb. 26, returning to Cooranbong same day, after speaking in the tent at 3 p.m. At her "Sunnyside" home most of March and April, meeting frequent speaking appointments, including speaking in the open air at Dora Creek and Martinsville; also busy with writing and many other matters. Took part in dedication of the main school building April 16. Again labored in Newcastle April 21-23 and May 19-21, and at Summer Hill and Stanmore in late May. Apparently at home most of the time during June, July, Aug., and early Sept., carrying her usual burdens.

Australian Union Conf. was held at the Avondale school July 6-25. E.G.W. was very ill during a week of that time, but spoke, seated, July 17. Spoke again July 22. With W.C.W. and wife drove to Maitland Sept. 8, to join Elders Starr and Daniells in search for place for camp meeting. Then took train for Strathfield for weekend. Returned to "Sunnyside" Sept. 10. Met appointments at Wallsend, Newcastle, in mid-Sept., and at Hamilton, Newcastle, Sept. 29-Oct. 2, when the new church was opened. Drove to Hornsby Junction with W.C.W. and several others Oct. 3 to investigate land being considered for San. site.

Labored in camp meeting in Toowoomba Oct. 13-22, and again visited San. site near Hornsby Junction in late Oct. Labored in camp meeting at Maitland Nov. 14-30, and apparently made another trip to Maitland later in Nov. This was one of the places she had seen in vision a year earlier pleading for light. E.G.W. had a great burden for the work there, and spent two or three weekends there in Dec. Also met several speaking appointments at Avondale during Dec.

1900

At "Sunnyside" home much exhausted as year began. Suffering pain in left eye, and writing with eye bound up. With Sara M. went to Summer Hill and then to San. farm for rest, Jan. 4-19. Neither got much rest! Was impressed to go to Maitland; woke Sara at 4 a. m. Jan. 19, took early train to Dora Creek Station, and that afternoon drove to Maitland for a busy weekend of meetings. Visited Maitland again Feb. 9-12. Left "Sunnyside" March 7 to labor in the camp meeting at Geelong, Victoria, March 8-23.

Impressed that she should soon return to America, and wrestled much in prayer before she decided to go. Spent a weekend in Melbourne area on return journey and spoke in N. Fitzroy church on Sabbath afternoon; reached "Sunnyside" March 27. Made no long trips during next four months, but was burdened with writing and her concern over many features of the work, both in Australia and America. Labored several weekends in Maitland, Hamilton, Summer Hill, and Parramatta. Dreaded giving up her pleasant home to go to America but was convinced she must, and in August was busy with preparations for the move. Sunday, Aug. 26, a fitting farewell service was held in the Cooranbong church, and on Aug. 29 she sailed from Sydney on the *S. S. Moana* with W.C.W. and family and Sara M. Reached San Francisco Friday p.m. Sept. 21, and spoke in the Oakland church Sabbath p.m.

Spent a few days in Oakland, house hunting, and went to St. Helena Sept. 27. At St. Helena San. learned of a home fully furnished that was for sale, surely the very place the Lord had prepared for her, and "Elmshaven" became her home until her death. While on board ship she had been visited "by the angel of the Lord" and given precious instruction and the assurance that the Lord had a place prepared for her.

Attended camp meeting at Napa, and during closing months of the year labored in St. Helena area, Oakland, San Francisco, Calistoga, and Healdsburg, and became settled in her new home, for which she was deeply grateful. *Christ's Object Lessons*, *Testimonies on Sabbath School Work,* and *Testimonies for the Church*, vol. 6, were published in 1900.

1901

Returned to "Elmshaven" Dec. 31, 1900, and was quite ill for 3 weeks. Spoke in San. chapel Jan. 19. Burdened with writing—preparing books for publication. Started journey to Battle Creek for Gen. Conf. about March 6. Spoke in Los Angeles church Sabbath, March 9; became very ill in p.m. and lost consciousness for hours, but the Lord sustained her and she continued her journey, accompanied by W.C.W., Sara M., and others.

Spent a few days with her son Edson on the *Morning Star* at Vicksburg, and spoke on Sabbath and Sunday, when the church was dedicated; at Nashville she met Emma White; also spoke to Nashville believers; spent Sabbath and Sunday in Chicago, where she spoke on Sabbath and to the medical students on Sunday. From Chicago proceeded to B.C. for the G.C. session where she bore many burdens. "The Conference was a time of taxing labor for me." Following the Conference, spent a few days in Indianapolis, to help meet a difficult situation there—the holy flesh fanaticism; spent May 6 and 7 with church and San. workers in Des Moines, Iowa; May 8 and 9 in College View, Neb.; met appointments in Denver and Boulder, Colo. Labored in Upper Columbia camp meeting in Waitsburg, Wash., visited Walla Walla, and labored in N. Pacific camp meeting at Portland, Ore.

Returned to Oakland in time to meet Elders Irwin and Salisbury before they sailed for Australia May 30; thence to her "Elmshaven" home, very worn and suffering from a cold and sore throat. Attended camp meeting in Oakland June 5-23 and spoke 11 times. Also labored in camp meeting in Los Angeles in Aug. and on return trip stopped in Oakland and attended meetings of Pacific Press Board. Met speaking appointments in Healdsburg (including attendance at teachers' institute), Santa Rosa, and Petaluma, as well as in St. Helena area, during next few months.

Convicted that she had work to do in the East, left for New York Nov. 6, arriving there Nov. 11, and labored for nearly two weeks (including an appointment in Trenton, N.J.); spent some time in late Nov. and early Dec. in So. Lancaster, took treatments at San.; there were many calls for her labors, but, not being well, she apparently went direct from So. Lancaster to Nashville, to labor in So. Union Conf. session Jan. 3-12. Reached Nashville about mid-December.

1902

In Nashville and very ill as year began but was greatly blessed in special season of prayer in her behalf. Too feeble to participate in the Union Conf. meetings. Left Nashville about Jan. 12. Had several hours in Chicago and was taken by auto to Hinsdale San. for treatment. Reached her "Elmshaven" home Jan. 17, thankful that her life had been spared. Gradually improved in health in following weeks, and continued her writing (even while so ill in Nashville). Tested her voice by speaking a short while in Calistoga church March 15.

Visited Oakland for "an important council meeting" late in April. Spoke several times in camp meeting at Petaluma June 5-15; also filled several local speaking appointments. Spent Sept. 10 in Oakland, en route south; stopped at Santa Barbara to counsel re establishing a sanitarium and restaurant there; went to San Fernando to see a property that might be purchased for school site. Labored in camp meeting at Los Angeles, Sept. 12-21. Also visited other possible locations for sanitarium work.

Left L.A. Sept. 24 for San Diego, and drove to Paradise Valley to see prospective sanitarium site there, spoke to believers Sabbath forenoon and Sunday p.m. Returned to L.A. and visited Pasadena, where Dr. Evans had opened treatment rooms; was present at opening of school in San Fernando. Labored in camp meeting at Fresno in early Oct. and returned home about Oct. 13. Burdened with much writing, and her mind occupied with many matters during remainder of year. *Testimonies for the Church*, vol. 7, and *Manual for Canvassers* were published in 1902.

1903

At home busily writing and laboring locally much of the year. Deeply distressed over conditions in Battle Creek, and the falling of God's judgments. (The B.C. San. had burned Feb. 18, 1902, and the RH Pub. House on Dec. 30, 1902.) Had a vision of what *might have been* at the 1901 Gen. Conf. Labored in GC Ses-

sion in Oakland (and pre-Conf. meetings), March 23-
April 13. Carried burdens that taxed her strength severely. Was very weak following the conference, but
continued to write, and prayed that there might be a
"humbling of proud hearts before the Lord."

Attended closing exercises of Healdsburg College
and gave Baccalaureate sermon May 30. Met with College Board June 6 and 7. Spoke to teachers assembled in
teachers' institute at Healdsburg in Aug., and again
visited Healdsburg and spoke before Calif. Conf. Committee, College Board, and Calif. Med. Miss. and
Benev. Assoc. Greatly distressed over influence of *Living Temple* and Dr. Kellogg's apostasy. *Education* was
published in 1903.

1904

At "Elmshaven" in early months, writing as able,
and meeting local appointments. Attended second biennial session of Pacific Union Conf. in Healdsburg,
March 18-28. Left St. Helena April 18, with Sara M.
and Maggie Hare. Stopped in Mt. View to see land
chosen for PPPA, then took train for overland journey,
via L.A. Reached Washington April 24, and located in
a comfortable house with her workers. Busy with coun-
selling, speaking appointments, and writing. Gave
dedicatory address for Memorial Church, May 7. Attended 2nd biennial session of Lake Union Conf. in
Berrien Springs, Mich., May 17-25.

Went with Edson to Nashville; very weary, but
spoke on Sabbath in Nashville church. Ill and unable to
do much writing; spent a week on *S.S. Morning Star*

with Edson and Emma. Visited in Graysville and Huntsville June 17-22; left Nashville for Washington July 6 and labored there in much weakness until August 10. Spent a few days at San. in Phila. and spoke in two tents pitched there. Spent 2 weeks in New England San., Melrose, Mass., taking treatments, speaking to nurses and helpers, and in the camp meeting a mile away. Improved in strength. Wrote often to Marian D., ill in St. Helena San. Visited Middletown, Conn., and spoke 4 times at So. New Eng. camp meeting. (Marian D. died Oct. 25.)

In B.C. San. Sept. 6-8; spoke to patients, nurses, and helpers, and in Tabernacle. Attended latter part of camp meeting in Omaha, Neb., and G.C. Committee Council in College View, then returned for appointments in B.C. Sept. 28-Oct. 3. Left for Calif. Oct. 3, stopped in Reno for Sabbath, and reached her "Elmshaven" home Oct. 9. Left Oct. 28 for So. Calif. Met appointments in Fresno on Sabbath, then spent a few days in Hanford and assisted in meetings there and in Lemoore and Armona. In L.A. weekend of Nov. 3-7, and spoke in tent Sabbath and Sunday. In San Diego Nov. 7-28, ill and unable to do much speaking, but pleased with progress in preparing San. for occupancy. Visited Glendale San., Redlands, Riverside, San Fernando, and L.A. in early Dec., and returned to "Elmshaven" about Dec. 19 or 20. *Testimonies for the Church*, vol. 8, was published in 1904.

1905

Attended portion of Bookmen's Convention in

Mt. View Jan. 19-25, and spoke a number of times. Busy with final work on *MH* and *9T*, and burdened to prepare many things already written, for publication. Granddaughter Ella was married to D. E. Robinson May 1. Left May 3 for Washington, to attend G.C. session. Accompanied by W.C.W. and wife and Maggie Hare. Reached D.C. May 10; spoke at opening meeting of session and 10 times during session; also in Takoma Park church June 3. Left D.C. for Calif. June 7. Stopped 10 days in So. Calif. and joined in counsel re Loma Linda property; also visited San Diego and Paradise Valley San., and Glendale.

Attended San Jose camp meeting, and spoke 5 times. Returned to "Elmshaven" about July 4; exceedingly busy with writing. Attended So. Calif. camp meeting in August; visited Loma Linda, Glendale, and Paradise Valley San., speaking and counseling at each place. Returned home to "Elmshaven" about Sept. 21, and spent remaining months of 1905 writing and meeting speaking appointments locally. Greatly burdened with the various interests of the work and with her writing; anxious to prepare for printing much valuable counsel in her files. Troubled by thought that she might die and leave important work unfinished. *The Ministry of Healing* was published in 1905.

1906

At home, busy with writing as year began. Deeply burdened over Battle Creek and many other matters. Often in night visions seemed to be in meetings giving counsel, or witnessing scenes that impressed her to write. Left St. Helena April 12 for So. Calif. Spoke 30 minutes at dedication of Loma Linda San., Sunday, April 15. That night had vision of destruction of cities. Attended 3rd session of So. Calif. Conf. Spoke in L.A. church Wed., April 18; learned of San Francisco earthquake. Spoke in San Diego church Sabbath, April 21, and at dedication of Paradise Valley San. April 24. Returned to Loma Linda to meet with brethren to consider health food business in So. Calif.

Left for home May 2; nearing San Jose saw effects of earthquake; stopped off at Mt. View and remained over Sabbath to counsel with Pacific Press Board. Distressed to see fallen walls of publishing house, but thankful no workers were killed. Was specially strengthened to speak on Sabbath. En route home spent some time driving through San Francisco and viewing the ruins left by the earthquake. Our church still standing. At home most of the time from early May till end of year.

Distressed over Dr. Kellogg's attitude and that of A. T. Jones; also over the false charge that others manipulated her writings. Though ill and weak and perplexed, did much important writing. Attended camp meeting in Oakland in July, and spoke several times. (Sabbath, July 21, word reached the campground that the Pacific Press had been destroyed by fire.) Visited Oakland Aug. 16-20, and spoke in the tent, and Aug. 31-Sept. 2 was again in Oakland, where she spoke to union service for the area churches. Made two more visits to Oakland in September to fill speaking appointments, and also attended stockholders' meeting and general council meeting at Pacific Press. Oct. 18-21 visited Oakland "for the fifth time since the close of the July camp meeting." In Nov. spent two weekends in San Francisco-Oakland area, and another in Dec. Nov. 6 wrote: "My work is nearly completed, . . . My books will testify when my voice shall no longer be heard."

1907

At home devoting herself to writing during early months of 1907. In Oakland Feb. 15-18; united with Elder and Mrs. Haskell in the work there; had to bear plain testimony and meet difficult situation. In March wrote of the heavy weight of responsibility she was bearing that no one could understand. Felt *alone*. Left with W.C.W., Sara M., and Dores R. April 18 for So. Calif. Labored at San Fernando school, Loma Linda, San Diego, and Paradise Valley San., San Pasqual, Escondido, Los Angeles, and Glendale through late April and first 3 weeks of May. Spent May 23-27 in Merced, laboring in camp meeting. Reached home May 27, after 6 weeks' absence. In spite of weakness and suffering, had filled her appointments. Felt "the power of the Spirit" imparted to her whenever she stood before the people to speak.

Camped on grounds and labored in camp meeting in St. Helena June 20-30, and was very ill following that meeting. Spoke 20 minutes at dedication of St. Helena San., Oct. 20. (Dedication of new hospital building.) Left home Oct. 27 for another visit to So. Calif. Labored in medical convention in Loma Linda, and at Paradise Valley San.; also in Los Angeles and Glendale. Returned home about Dec. 24. Concerning this period in So. Calif. she wrote: "The burden was upon me night and day." "It was a long and wearisome journey, and I was worn with continual anxiety."

1908

At home busily writing as year began, though much worn from her labors in So. Calif. as 1907 closed. Spoke twice during Union Conf. session in San chapel in Jan. Received and counseled visitors; rode out when able. Spent ten days in Oakland during Bible Institute, and spoke six times (in March). Visited Lake County a few days in April. Spoke several times at Lodi camp meeting, May 1-10, and returned home ill with cold, and weary. Feeling the pressure of much writing, and that she must spend more time out-of-doors. Spoke six times at camp meeting in Melrose, Oakland, in early June "with as great clearness and power as in early times."

Left home Aug. 5 for So. Calif. Delayed 8 hours in intense heat because of wreck. Reached L.A. Aug. 7 and labored in camp meeting. Weak and ill, was taken to Glendale San. for treatment Aug. 16. Visited Paradise Valley San. Aug. 24-27, then labored at Loma Linda, and returned home in early Sept., after nearly five weeks' absence. Apparently stopped in Oakland over Sabbath on return trip. Laboring in weariness and feeling greatly the pressure to prepare matter for printing; searching her writings for that which she desired to have published. Remarkably strengthened to address a meeting of the Medical Convention in St. Helena in late Oct. All felt presence of Holy Spirit, and following this meeting her health improved and courage was renewed.

During November made weekend trips to Sebastopol, Healdsburg, and Berkeley, and was strengthened to speak. The "strange work" of Bro. and Sr. Mackin had to be met at this time. Study was being given to the removal of the college from Healdsburg to a more desirable location, and Buena Vista property was under consideration. E.G.W. joined in study of this problem.

1909

Pressed with physical suffering and many anxieties over the work, but continuing her writing, reading of Mss., etc., eager to complete matter for books. Spoke 3 times in Oakland in Feb. at annual session of Calif. Conf. Left home April 5, with W.C.W., Sara M., and Minnie H., for G.C. session in Takoma Park. Spent April 7 and 8 at Paradise Valley San., and addressed the patients. At Loma Linda spoke to patients and members "gathered under the pepper trees" on Sabbath. In College View, Neb., April 16-20, and spoke several times. Visited institutions in Nashville area, in Huntsville, Ala., and Asheville, N. C., speaking in each place.

Reached Washington May 3, after a "long journey" in which she "labored constantly." Continued to labor "constantly" before the session (May 13-June 6), during the session, and following the session. Met appointments in Philadelphia following G.C. session; also in New York City and Newark, N. J. Rested a few days in So. Lancaster, then labored in camp meeting at

Nashua, N.H. Visited Concord and saw property secured for Jewish workers, then returned to So. Lancaster for a few days before laboring in camp meeting at Portland, Me.

Spent a few days at New England San. in Melrose, Mass., then started on long homeward journey, stopping for appointments en route at Buffalo, N. Y., Battle Creek, camp meeting at Three Rivers, Mich., Wabash Valley San. at Lafayette, Ind., Elgin, Ill. camp meeting, Hinsdale, Ill., Madison, Wis. camp meeting, Iowa camp meeting at Nevada, Iowa, Kansas camp meeting at Council Grove, Kan., Eastern Colo. camp meeting at Boulder, Colo., and Salt Lake City, Utah. Suffered severely from failing heart in high altitude of the Rockies, and was transferred in wheel chair at Oakland pier and Vallejo Junction. Reached home Sept. 9, after five months absence.

Sept. 10 went in her easiest carriage to see the Angwin property, which had been purchased for the college. Attended latter part of Calif. camp meeting at Fruitvale, Sept. 13-16. Spent a few days at the new college site in late Sept. and early Oct., and took part in dedication of the school Sept. 29. Labored in Bible Institute in San Jose in mid-Oct., and in workers' institute in Lodi Nov. 5-14; also in Week of Prayer at Mt. View and Oakland in mid-Dec. *Testimonies for the Church*, vol. 9, was published in 1909.

1910

Much occupied in reading articles and book matter in preparation, as well as writing. Labored in Union

Conf. session at Mt. View Jan. 24-30; attended annual
session of Calif. Conf. in Lodi Feb. 1-6, and workers'
institute in Oakland latter half of March. Labored in
Glendale, Los Angeles, Loma Linda, San Fernando,
San Diego, and Paradise Valley San. from end of March
till mid-May. Reached home much worn. Labored in
camp meeting at Napa in late June and in camp meeting
in Berkeley in August; visited Angwin and spoke to the
students a few times during the year. Busily writing on
Old Testament history.

1911

Apparently at home, laboring as able, during Jan.,
Feb., and most of March. It seems to have been during
this period that she had 23 X-ray treatments for a black
spot on her forehead, which was entirely removed by
the treatments. Writing on the life of Paul. Left in late
March for So. Calif., and attended Loma Linda Board
meeting in early April, and met other speaking appointments. Also labored in Riverside, San Fernando,
Paradise Valley San., Glendale, and Los Angeles. Returned home late in April and spoke in San. chapel
Sabbath, April 29; also at P.U.C. May 20, St. Helena
May 27, and again at P.U.C. June 10.

Labored in camp meeting in Oakland July 6-16.
Working hard to complete *The Acts of the Apostles.*
Attended camp meeting in Long Beach, Calif, Aug.
10-20. Was wonderfully sustained when she gave her
last talk at the camp meeting, to a very large audience.
"I felt that the everlasting arms were underneath me,"
she wrote. Made a trip to Loma Linda at the end of Oct.

and spent a few weeks there, attending important meetings. W.C.W. had been in the East for some time, and she met him in L.L. at this time. *The Acts of the Apostles* was published late in 1911.

1912

Working as able on a book to take its place between *PP* and *DA*. The material, already written, needed to be put into shape. "When this book is completed, I shall feel that my work is finished," she wrote. Longed for a visit from Edson and Emma, and longed to visit Portland, Me., once more. Left mid-March or a little earlier to attend important meetings in So. Calif.—Ministerial Institute, Union Conf. session, C.M.E. Constituency meeting. Gave several discourses, both in L.A. and Loma Linda, the last one reported being on April 18.

Spoke to teachers and students at P.U.C. May 4. Conserving most of her strength for work on the book on OT, from the time of Solomon to Christ. Spoke again at P.U.C. Sept. 7. At Loma Linda again Nov. 6-Dec. 6. During Week of Prayer spoke in Calistoga one Sabbath and at P.U.C. one Sabbath.

1913

At "Elmshaven," maintaining her interest in the work, and laboring to complete certain writings. "I am getting old, but I am doing all that I can to glorify God," she wrote. Wrote two messages for the General Conference in session in Takoma Park in May.

Had several interviews with leading workers; spoke a few times locally. *Counsels to Parents, Teachers, and Students* was published in 1913.

1914

Visited by her son, James Edson, for several weeks in spring of 1914. June 14, wrote "The Victorious Life"—last writing before her death. TM 516-520. August 15, interview with W.C.W. reported. Ms. 12, 1914. September 8, interview with Dr. Thomason reported. Ms. 10, 1914. Dec. 23, one of her copyists wrote to W.C.W. about his mother. LS 436, 437.

In a conversation held Dec. 2 recalled an incident of many years earlier. Early in December heard voices in the night season, crying: "Advance! Advance!" Longed to be active, but realized her waning strength. Her prayer of December 26. LS 441.

1915

Sabbath, Feb. 13, met with the accident that hastened her death; fell as she was entering her study, sustaining a fracture of the left femur. PUR Feb. 25, 1915. March 17 E.G.W. was visited by a number of leading workers; she was "pleased to meet these old friends." March 31, on W.C.W.'s return from Loma Linda, when he asked how she was feeling, she responded, "I am getting along pretty well—in rather a hard way."—PUR April 15, 1915.

The end to this great life came at 3:40 o'clock Friday afternoon, July 16, when Ellen White fell asleep in Jesus, "as quietly and peacefully as a weary child going to her rest."—PUR July 22, 1915. *Gospel Workers* (new and revised edition) and *Life Sketches of Ellen G. White* were published in 1915.

APPENDIX C*

G. B. STARR'S COMMENTS AT ELLEN WHITE'S ELMSHAVEN FUNERAL SERVICE

IT is my privilege to speak of some of the phases of the life of Sister White. I have known her nearly 40 years, and Mrs. Starr has known her over 50 years. We have learned from her own lips the story of her early conversion at the age of 13 years, from doubt and darkness into light and special love for the person of Jesus Christ. I think I have never heard any other person speak of love for Jesus, personal love, as I have heard her speak. Many times, in large congregations, I have heard her break forth in the expression, "Jesus, I love You; I *love* You, I LOVE You!" Some here know that; they have heard it; and it has thrilled the audience. We have felt the influence of that love for Jesus.

I believe it is a splendid thing for us to emulate, not only to have faith in a general way, but faith in Jesus and in His love. Her entire life was devoted to winning others to love Him and serve Him with their hearts.

In her writings are to be found what I consider the clearest, most forceful, simple, earnest, presentation of the gospel to be found in any writings, outside of the Scriptures themselves. The language in her writings is of the most attractive, simple, and forceful style. Now, I will leave you to judge that for yourselves, that it is

---

* Ellen White died Friday, July 16, 1915. Three funeral services followed. On Sunday afternoon, July 18, a funeral service was conducted on the lawn at her "Elmshaven" home. The next day a funeral was conducted at the Richmond camp meeting. On Sabbath, July 24, the third and largest funeral service was held at Battle Creek, Michigan.

attractive, elevating, forceful, and there is nothing to be found like it in the world. I have never seen anyone whose writings at all imitated her writings. In the little book *Steps to Christ*—I had the privilege of reading that book in the manuscript, and she asked several of us to advise what should be done with it. "Why," we said, "put it into every language as soon as possible, for it is the simplest, clearest guide in the saving faith of Jesus we have ever read." That book has been translated into [many] languages.

I saw a table with a complete set of her published books on it. I think it is under the trees on the other side of the house. I think it should be nearer. It makes a number of volumes that is quite surprising.

As I looked at her the other day, as I clasped her hand and bade her good-bye, I thought, "That hand has written more gospel exhortation and precious things than perhaps any other human hand. I have studied the writings of a good many, but I know of no one who is as diligent as she was, getting up at 2, 3, or 4 o'clock in the morning, and working until after sundown. She retired very early, that was her habit, and then early in the morning she would arise and begin her writing. You would find her, like all the prophets, rising early and doing her work.

I have seen her, I think, under nearly all the circumstances under which you meet a friend. We had the privilege of traveling with her in Michigan, and then of accompanying her to Australia, living in her home, seeing her under all the circumstances of home life, and, in addition, with the burdens of the world's work that she loved upon her; and I want to testify today that Mrs. Starr and I consider her one of the most constant, faithful Christians that we have met in our lives. I do not say that in order to praise her here today, but I believe it from the heart; I have reason to know it; I know it personally.

She has been a great help to me personally. She has not written me flattering letters when I have been in the mission fields, in Queensland and other places, but she has written me very earnest words of counsel that have been very profitable to me in my life and ministry.

I wish to note her character as a friend, and I am sure that all who know her here will verify what I say. Her remembrance of names of individuals was very remarkable. She never seemed to forget a person whom she met in any part of the world. She carried them on her heart and in her prayers. Her faithfulness in friendship was very marked, extending through trial and temptation. As the little boy at school said when asked the meaning of friendship, "A true friend is one who knows all about you and loves you just the same," so we can say of her, that though she knew the failings of her friends very well, she loved them just the same, and prayed for them and labored for them just the same.

Another word about her character: I regarded her as one of the sturdiest characters I ever met. I can compare her life only to the sturdy oak that meets the wind and bears its severest pressure; or the mountain that laughs at the storm. She met trial and opposition from those who ought to have been friendly; and she met it in the kindest, sweetest spirit, but with the firmest determination to conquer, always conquer. I never knew her to be conquered. Her faith in God was invincible in this country, or any other country. Under circumstances that would have swamped the faith of many, she triumphed under trial.

Just a word further about her sickness. It has been her lot, as Brother Loughborough remarked, to suffer more than the ordinary Christian. God permitted it, and she—I think I will let her speak for herself as to how she regarded it. I have a statement here from her own writings that I will read:

"I do not now expect to be lifted above all infirmities and tribulations, and to have an unruffled sea on the journey heavenward. I expect trials, losses, disappointments, and bereavements"—and she had them, two children and her husband buried where she will soon be buried by their side, in Michigan; she had her trials in that way, and in other ways—"but I have the Saviour's promise, 'My grace is sufficient for thee.'

"My sickness has taught me my own weakness, and my Saviour's patience and love, and His power to save. When passing sleepless nights, I have found hope and comfort in considering the forbearance and tenderness of Jesus toward His weak, erring disciples, and remembering that He is still the same—unchangeable in mercy, compassion, and love. He sees our weakness; He knows how we lack faith and courage; yet He does not cast us off. He is pitiful and of tender compassion toward us."

About six weeks ago we called on her, and she said, "When were you in last to see me?"

"Just last Sabbath afternoon," I replied.

"Oh, yes," she said, "I forgot." And then she turned to us and said: "We all have our weaknesses and our forgetfulnesses, but if we correct them they add strength to our characters and do not belittle us." Now that, you see, is similar to her statement that Christ reveals His tender compassion through suffering.

Speaking of her death, she said: "I may fall at my post before the Lord shall come; but when all that are in their graves shall come forth, I shall, if faithful" —and she was faithful—"see Jesus, and be made like Him. Oh, what joy, unspeakable, to see Him whom we love—to see Him in His glory who so loved us that He gave Himself for us—to behold those hands once pierced for our redemption, stretched out to us in blessing and welcome!" Those are triumphant words, aren't they?

Now, while here, she sang considerably. I want to read you one verse of one song that she very much delighted in. We heard her singing it the other morning, as we were at the bottom of the stairs. We said, "Who is that singing?" and they said, "That is Sister White." Here is what she sang: "We have heard from the bright, the holy land, We have heard, and our hearts are glad; For we were a lonely pilgrim band, And weary, and worn, and sad. They tell us the pilgrims have a dwelling there—No longer are homeless ones; And we know that the goodly land is fair, Where life's pure river runs."

Then she would omit two verses and she would use

the last part of the last verse as sort of a chorus, and would repeat it over and over again. This was her chorus: "We'll be there, we'll be there, in a little while, We'll join the pure and the blest; We'll have the palm, the robe, the crown, And forever be at rest." She would repeat that again and again.

Some have asked a question about her position among us. She was never elected to any office. She never desired any office. When a person would speak of any particular work, she would say, "My work to which God has called me is to be His messenger," and that was her highest desire, to be the messenger of Jesus Christ.

In bidding her good-bye two weeks ago today, she said to us—as Brother White spoke to her, (she seemed to be very bright that morning), he said, "Mother, Brother and Sister Starr have come to bid you good-bye." She said she was very glad to see us again. I said, "We are glad to find you so bright this morning." This was her reply: "I am glad you find me thus, and I wish to tell you that it is bright inside." And then she added, "I have not had many mournful days, have I?" "No, Sister White," I said, "not in all your life, because you have risen above them." "Yes," said she, "my heavenly Father has planned it all for me, and He knows when it will end, and I am determined not to murmur."

I felt that that was a great triumph—and she did triumph. May the Lord help us to follow in her steps. Then I said to her, "I can only tell you, Sister White, what you wrote us in one of your last letters. You said,

'The shadows are lengthening' "—and I thought of it just now. She said, "Brother Starr, the shadows are lengthening, and we are nearing home. We will soon be home, and then we will talk it all over together in the kingdom of God."

APPENDIX D

J. N. LOUGHBOROUGH
LETTER TO LIDA SCOTT

Sanitarium, California
Sept. 20, 1921

Lida F. Scott
Madison, Tennessee

DEAR Sister Scott:
Your letter of September 8, enclosing numbers 1, 4, and 5 of the Madison leaflets, duly received. Thank you for the leaflets and your remembrance of me. Your letter caused these thoughts.

We are apt to think of our friends, whom we have not seen in a long time, as we last saw them. So I suppose my friends a distance from here think of me as when they saw me years ago when I was actively at work all over the country, and even making a trip in my ministerial work all around the world. It may be a surprise to such to learn that I was eighty-nine years of age the 26th of last January, and that I have been off this hill on which this sanitarium stands only three times in three and one-half years.

I thank you for your invitation to attend your Missionary Volunteer convention October 7-9. Although I cannot come in the flesh, I can assure you, as Paul did the Colossians, "Though I be absent in the flesh, yet am I with you in the spirit, joying and beholding your order, and the stedfastness of your faith in Christ."

I thank the Lord I am free from bodily pains, but am only feeble with age. If I cannot get about in public labors as formerly, I thank God that, as Sister White said to a sister who had been an active Bible worker when in health but was unable thus longer to work, "Sister, you can work now as well as formerly—you can pray for those who have health to be actively engaged in the great harvest field of labor."

I have watched with intense interest the work of Brother Sutherland since being privileged to be with him a short time years ago when he was in the Battle Creek College, when I gave a few talks there. Then I was glad to see him move out in the plan of which we had been told, that our educational centers should have lands for culture, etc., connected with them. I watched with prayerful interest his work in connection with establishing the college at Berrien Springs, Michigan.

Then especially have my mind and prayers been associated with his labors in the South in harmony with instruction as to what should be done there. Be assured, fellow workers, that my mind and faith are with you in your earnest work to do what the Lord has told us should be done. May the Lord's blessing be especially in the deliberation of the convention, will be my prayer while you are thus assembled.

> Yours in the blessed gospel hope,
> J. N. Loughborough

Index

Page

A

B

C

Camp meetings

Cancer,
Cause

Character

Charity,
Children

Church

Churches,
Cities,
Claims of Jesus,
Companion,

D

E

F

G

H

I

J

L

M

N

O

P

R

Robbery
   of God, is not impulsive but a well-considered plan..........108
   recorded in heaven against many church members...........108

S

Sadness, Lord would not have us grieve in......................159
Sanctuary, heavenly, correct understanding of
      ministration in...78
Satan, no excuse for becoming more like 67
Self-denial and sacrifice, God blessed those who
      advanced by..25
Self-discipline, age no excuse for relaxing 67
Selfish act, Christ's life not marred by one 89
Sentinels, aged, cannot afford to let drop out of sight 17
Service
   older workers not released from...................................31
   unselfish, no act of, however small, is ever lost...............153
Share, each believer has a, in trust given to first disciples 100
"Shut-in religion," avoid 74
Sin, none worse than bringing grief to aged parents 54
Smith, Uriah 16
   name to be retained as leading editor of *Review* 20
Solomon
   apostasy of, should warn every soul 180
   case of, is before us as a beacon of warning 181
   connection with God, lost when became older 181
   dishonored God by choosing to be controlled by lust 180
   life of, is full of warning......................................177
   mistook license for liberty 179
   repentance of, sincere, but evil example could not be
      undone 182
   repented and found help..178
Standard-bearers
   aged, far from being useless......................................18
      not to be loaded down with burdens 45
   experiences of to strengthen young workers.......................31
   to go from place to place for meetings...........................37

T

U

V

W